See what others have said about Peter A Hubbard's 'Tears' trilogy

**The US Review of Boo**ks *"The result is a masterclass of investigative acumen, psychological insight, and global coordination."*

**HOLLYWOOD Book Reviews** *"The writing style has a literary structure that crafts poignant visuals drawing you into the intensity of the moment, such as a mushroom cloud described with sooty grey contrails against the blue sky and compared to a canvas from Dante's Inferno."*

**Pacific Book Review** *"The action and intensity of the plot balanced out the depth of relationship building that occurred with this cast of characters, from the protagonist's own traumatic past that brought her into the field and into a life of government and military service, to the tragedies which befell the children who would become the faces behind the movement which these terrorists fuel their campaign with."*

**Christina Avina-Professional Book Reviewer** *"As a fan of this genre, I was enthralled with the author's writing and was even more moved by the rich themes developed in this book, including the heavy look at the morality behind those who are radicalized or brainwashed into committing such heinous actions after having witnessed or experiencing their own brand of injustice early on in life. The cycle of violence and destruction plays a major role in this thriller."*

peterahubbardbooks.com

# THE HANDBOOK OF
# PERSONAL POWER

Dr. Peter A. Hubbard

Published in the United States of America

Brilliant Books Literary
137 Forest Park Lane Thomasville
North Carolina 27360 USA

ISBN:
Paperback: 979-8-88945-157-0
Ebook: 979-8-88945-158-7

Mollydookers
ADVERTISING I DESIGN I DIGITAL I PRINT

Look for the psychological thrillers by Peter A Hubbard

The Tears of Hope
The Tears of Wonder
The Tears of Joy
The Island of Tears

This book is dedicated to Lyla Brooks, Agent extraordinaire, without whom this would not have been possible.

.

"A Book
that will quickly
and easily show you
how to get
all the wealth,
all the prosperity,
all the success,
and all the personal power
you could ever want."


By Dr. Peter A Hubbard
Melbourne, 2022

This may well be the most brilliant,
stimulating, engrossing book
of its type ever written.
But no matter how good it might be,
it is of absolutely no value
whatsoever
if you do nothing with it.
It is up to you,
it is always up to you,
and it always will be up to you.
As a wise man once asked,
when stimulating a thoughtful student,
"Give me but ten words
that can change the Universe,
conquer the Stars,
and deliver to Mankind
all the promises of God,
in but two letters each."
The student pondered the problem
for three thousand years,
or so it is said,
and then proclaimed for all to hear,
"IF IT IS TO BE, IT IS UP TO ME."

In the next three thousand years,
everything changed, and yet nothing has changed.

# THE ONE PAGE YOU MUST ABSOLUTELY READ

In every great book, there tends to be that one special paragraph, that one outrageous sentence, or that one sizzling page that sets your mind on fire, turns your legs to jelly, and brings a sparkle to your eyes.

Most of the rest of the book you relegate to distant, sometimes fond, memory.

But that one mind-snapping passage of words that sets your heart racing, that snaps your mind into high gear, you remember forever.

You laugh about it. You joke about it. You tell everyone you meet about it. And mostly, because they haven't read the book, or they don't think like you do, they never quite get the same point!

It feels frustrating, you get mad, and then you realise that some of the things you see, and much of what you believe, is yours, and yours alone. Other people don't see things exactly as you do.

And that's what the Handbook of Personal Power is all about.

It collates all the truly great things you can do to improve your ability to communicate with others; your ability to think and plan; and your ability to execute what it is you most want to do with both your personal and business life.

Through reading it, you will quickly and easily find all the hints and secrets you need to develop your wealth, your prosperity, your success, and your personal power.

Not everyone you know will read it the same way you do.

In fact, not everyone will even want to read it.

But if they do, it might just help them to change the way they see themselves, and help them to increase their awareness, and enhance their performance, and, just maybe, change their Life.

You can only try!

But just remember this very important secret - People only learn what they want to learn, when they want to learn it.

And just because someone does learn something, there's no guarantee that they will do anything with what they learn.

It's a bit like you trying to tell them how great that special passage in the book was - because they haven't been through the same process as you have, it affects them a different way.

And here's another great tip - When it comes to someone else's opinion, it's not necessarily right, it's not necessarily wrong, it's just different!

How important is it for you to remember that?

Absolutely vital!

Because how you come across to someone else is directly related to how much notice they think you are taking of them, and what they are saying!

And the influence of your personal power is limited by your ability to influence others. If they think you aren't listening to them, then they won't listen to you.

Getting people to listen to you is the key to personal wealth, prosperity, success, and power.

Being able to influence them in how they think, what they do, and when they do it, is crucial to your ultimate success. The Handbook of Personal Power will show you clearly what this is all about.

But remember this - what you do with these secrets will empower them to work for you, or not, as the case may be.

If you do nothing, expect nothing.

If you do something, expect something.

But if you take them into your heart and mind, taste them, and roll them around your brain box, get the feel for them, then use them wisely, you can expect to achieve great things with your life!

Personal wealth.

Personal prosperity.

Personal success.

Personal power.

And Personal happiness.

It's that sort of book.

And the really amazing thing is, the more you read this book, the more sure you will be that you know most of this stuff already! And in truth, you probably do.

Like anything good, and powerful, once started, the learning process will never be finished.

All the personal power, and all the good fortune, as always, is yours for the taking.

What you must do now,

is choose to take it!

# WHERE TO FIND EVERYTHING YOU NEED TO KNOW

This is usually called the Index Page,
but because we're heavily
into the development
of Personal Power, we'll call it

# THE ENERGY SOURCE

# CONTENTS

This is a complete short story, designed to help you get everything you have learned so far into perspective. It's different, a little scary, and you might not like it at first.
But hang in there, because the rewards will be great!

# THE TEN COMMANDMENTS OF PERSONAL POWER

A very quick way to grasp
what you must know
to realise your fullest potential.
Now, no one ever said that
it would be this easy, did they?

If you're in a real hurry, and you need the power now, then comprehend these Ten Commandments and be on your way. But be warned, real power, like any energy source, often bites the careless hand that holds it!

If you want the maximum personal power, then you must change.

True personal power requires great love, of yourself and of all others.

In losing respect for others, you lose a measure of self-respect, and diminish your personal power.

No one can, or wants to, develop your personal power for you.

You can replenish your personal power by doing new and different things, and by avoiding repetitive habits.

You can always quit and run away, but you can never run away from yourself. The process of quitting quickly diminishes your personal power.

Where there's a will, there's a way. Just by deciding to do something, you empower your intellect, and your personal power swells and builds.

True personal power comes from within, and is directly proportional to the purity of your soul.

Personal power is fuelled by positive, right actions.

Personal power is destroyed by negative, wrong actions.

Developing true personal power is like awakening a sleeping giant, or surviving a 1,000 bomber raid on your mind. It is a "shocking" experience, because it tends to set your imagination and your intuitive abilities on fire, which motivates you to great heights. There is simply nothing you can't do if you develop your personal power to its fullest potential.

Nothing.

So what is "Personal Power"?

Personal (individual, private, your own, secret, and special) power (force, control, influence, authority, direction, and mastery) is the sum total of all your experience, of all your learning, and of all your abilities. It is available to all, but accepted by few.

It's what makes the difference between being rich (affluent, wealthy, and comfortable), having true prosperity (fame, prestige, status, and happiness), and being ultimately successful (efficient, prosperous, triumphant, victorious, distinguished, outstanding, and a star).

If you recognise any of these words as being what you seek for yourself, then get stuck into developing your personal power now. Don't wait another minute.

Wealth, prosperity, and success await you.

# THE SWIMMING POOL OF LIFE

Personal power is like a swimming pool
- it has definite limits,
beyond which you can't go.
Only you can choose to swim
in the deep end,
or wallow in the shallows.

Clint Eastwood, resplendent in his Airline Captain's uniform, four gold stripes proudly worn on each arm, struts purposefully into the cockpit of the Boeing 707.

"Good morning Captain," the Second Officer says, his neck held at a strange angle by the blunt barrel of a heavy automatic pistol. The terrorist smiles, his face a mass of scars and ugliness, and gestures for Clint to take his seat.

"Yes, good morning, my Captain," he says mockingly, resting back on the edge of the dead Flight Engineer's table. "Now, if you wouldn't mind, get us airborne as quickly as you can." Clint squints manfully at the camera, settles into his seat, then turns to his Co-pilot.

"Let's get this rolling," he says through clenched teeth, pushing the four throttles to the firewall. The big jet stutters, trembles, then slowly begins to move as the power of the flame spewing engines surges through the airframe.

In a matter of seconds, the jet is roaring down the runway at over 100 knots, nibbling at the air, getting ready to fly. For some reason, call it instinct if you will, the Co-pilot is alerted by Clint's decided lack of airline procedure, and casually asks out of the corner of his mouth, "Have you ever flown an aircraft before, Captain?"

"Not a one," Clint replies, jamming his feet on the brakes, screwing the huge whale of an aircraft off into the grass verge. As all Hell breaks out in the cockpit, terrorist fighting Clint, Clint fighting the aircraft, the Co-pilot fighting everybody, we are left with the certain feeling that it sometimes takes just a little more than putting on the uniform, to acquire the necessary skills we need in life.

Luckily, all this happened in a movie, and, yes, the bad guys get shot to bits, the passengers are rescued, and Clint gets to carve another two or three notches on the handle of his 44 magnum pistol (the most powerful hand-gun in the world!).

Unfortunately, life is not a movie, with endless rehearsals, and the chance to do things over again and again, until they are perfect. And you can't just leave the bits you don't like out, as discards on the cutting room floor. Everything you do affects your soul, and leaves a residue of experience. Every bit of experience contributes either a positive or a negative value to the amount of personal power you are able to use.

Now experience, by itself, is like so much worthless baggage. You have to internalise the experience, and make it part of your truth, for you to get any real value out of anything you do. We've discussed this previously.

What has all this got to do with Clint pretending to be a jet pilot ? Or swimming pools?

Plenty.

Just as putting on the Captain's uniform didn't empower our hero to fly the plane, doing things for the sake of doing them will not empower you, unless you internalise the experience gained in the doing. Internalise (enclose, take in, make your own) the process, suck in and chew on the understanding, discard what you don't want, then keep all the good bits. That's how you develop your personal power. Not by striving for or wearing the mantle of recognition, but by obtaining the skills and the experience to do the job.

A swimming pool (a traditional one) has four sides, two of which are long, and two of which are short. A deep end and a shallow end, and sometimes a set of stairs allowing easy access. When the pool is empty, you have this huge hole in the ground, that always appears to be larger to the eye than it really is. If you should walk into the hole, an ominous creepy feeling pervades your mind, as the pool seems to dominate your spirit. The lower you go, the further into the pool, the more hollow your voice sounds, and the heavier the air feels.

All that changes when the pool is full. It's soul-tugging emptiness is hidden, and the natural buoyancy of the water helps you to float on the surface. You actually have to work hard at getting down to the bottom, and staying there, without some compensating weights to hold you down.

The hole is the same dimension, it still is as large as it seemed, but now the very nature of the pool has been altered by filling it with water - fulfilling its destiny, as it were. (Allowing it to be used for the purpose for which it was designed and built).

Empty, the pool looms as a discontented object, unfulfilled, lacking in purpose, and poses a danger to all.

Full, it sparkles with joy and fulfilment, encouraging participation, and revels in being used to its fullest extent.

Your soul suffers the same fate as the empty swimming pool whenever you deny it your truest endeavours. Take away its substance, deny it stimulation, reduce your experiential learning, and your soul takes on all the gloomy, despondent, pervading feeling of the huge empty hole in the ground.

But fill your soul with stimulation, new experiences, exquisite samples of your intellect and your skills, and it flourishes and provides an endless stream of energy to your internal batteries, fuelling your personal power.

Just as it is the empty hole in the ground that must be filled before the true purpose of the pool can be realised, the emptiness within you must also be filled so that you can achieve your true purpose.

Once in the pool, you have several choices. You can play, or you can swim "laps". You can swim between the short sides, or stream up and down between the long ones. You can splash around in the shallows, or power around in the deep end. You can swim underwater, until you need to breathe again, or you can stay on the top.

Or you can just sit quietly off to one side, and watch the wind and the sun play with the water, in peace and tranquillity.

The swimming pool is very much like life. There are many, many choices, and just as many ways to benefit from them, or not, as the case may be. The point is, it is your life to determine what you will do with it, but determine something you must. And it is always your choices that determine what your life will be.

If you choose to float on the surface of the pool, eventually you will have to either get out, or accept drowning. You have a limited amount of energy, that needs replenishing. Simply put, you can't float forever. And if you try, you diminish your life force progressively to the point beyond which it cannot sustain you any longer.

Like a self-fulfilling prophecy, if you choose to cruise through life, you rob yourself of the very essence you need to survive and prosper.

But if you float for a predetermined period of time, allow-Ing your mind and body to rest, you are taking advantage of one of the greatest benefits given to mankind.

The ability to actively choose to regulate the environment around you, to suit your purpose-designed activity. Deliberately, and skilfully.

If you choose to swim long laps, you create the environment within which you can condition your physical state, and enhance your intellect. Controlled physical exertion causes the chemical factory in your body to release millions of naturally beneficial stimulants, helping your body to grow and achieve its potential.

Because your body (the walls of the pool that contain your emptiness) is actively benefiting, your intellect is freed up to spark and refurbish, enhancing your creativity and your ambition. Feel good, act good, look good, and you will be good, at whatever you choose to do.

By choosing the long sides, you are setting your sights on the big target, the one that requires the greatest effort, and promises the greatest reward. And you are using your body to enhance your personal power, but not in a physical way. It is the synergy between the physical effort and your intellect that provides the stimulus for your personal power.

And you can't have one without the other.

If you splash around in the shallows, eventually you will become tired, and flop down, feeling heavy and discontented. The water is not able to support your weight, and you feel uncomfortable because you are neither in it nor on it. It's like indecision - it robs you of your power, because too much of your energy is being consumed trying to make up for what you haven't got control of.

If you choose to play in the deep end, then all of a sudden you can float (choice one), swim (choice two), dive to the bottom (choice three), do laps (choice four), or just play around with a combination of any of the possibilities (choice five). But you have to make a choice, or you will have to retreat, by getting out of the pool. If you don't, you will eventually drown.

The upshot of this is that if you focus on your goals of wealth, prosperity, success and personal power, but choose to muddle your way through, either the process or the attainment of your goals may well sink you - physically, or mentally. It isn't good enough to just jump into the deep end, you need to know what you are going to do once you are there. You need a strategy, and from this strategy, you must develop some tactics.

Strategy is simply knowing what to do when there is apparently nothing to do. Tactics is doing something when there is something to do. So first, the plan - what is the goal you are going to achieve? And then the action - how are you going to achieve it.

If you want all the personal power that you are capable of generating, you have to develop it like any other energy force - you need a container (your body and your intellect), you need a source (the learning and experiencing process), you need control (your wisdom and compassion), you need an outlet (an objective, or something and someone to focus your personal power on), and you need other people (to act as force-multipliers).

Your personal power will always be limited by something - the amount of energy available, the purity of your soul, the amount of experiential learning you have participated in, the state of your intellect, your ability to focus on your goals, and your willingness to actively choose and execute your strategies and tactics. Just like the pool can only ever hold a predetermined volume of sparkling water, so too your soul can only hold a predetermined quantity of purity.

The one single key to firstly achieving, obtaining, and then being able to use your personal power is locked solidly in your ability to understand other people. You must understand yourself, that is axiomatic to your success. But you must also totally understand other people, so that you can empower them to help you to achieve your great role in life.

By yourself, you are always limited by the extent to which you can influence your environment to achieve your objective. But with others actively helping you, you multiply your influence many times more than the sum total of the people involved in your effort.

To successfully encompass others in your life quest, you need to know certain things. You must learn what motivates them. Where they are in the development of their own personal power. What their goals in life are. And how you can foster, and help them to achieve, their fullest potential.

Imagine that you have chosen the long sides of the pool to swim between. Your strategy is to swim 10 kilometres. This means that you have chosen to go for the biggest goal in your life, the one that will take the greatest effort, and provide the greatest reward.

You dive in the deep end, and you commence a series of laps. If you have good people at each end, who can continue lapping the pool for you in relay-style, while you occasionally pause to catch your breath, then you will quickly start to achieve your goal. Without the good people at each end, you are limited by your personal energy, and your influence is restricted to what you can achieve by yourself. If you don't make the 10 k's, you fail. You do not achieve your strategy.    When you falter, and start to sink, your achievement is coloured by what you have limited yourself by, and the limitations of your tactics. Your failure bruises your soul, depletes your personal power, and quenches your thirst for taking giant strides.

Not achieving your goal is far worse than never striving to attain it. When you choose to do something, you are making a commitment to yourself to execute a strategy to the fullest of your ability. If you believe that you cannot achieve it by yourself, then you are honour-bound to involve as many others as you need to see you through, because you must always be true to yourself!

The greatest salesman in the world is only as successful as the number of people who consent to buy from him or her. Likewise, you will only achieve your goals if you learn how to involve the skills and abilities of other people in what you choose to do, should it be beyond the limits of a normal man or woman.

Back to the pool. To get good people to stand at each end, swim laps for you on demand, and help you to achieve your goal, is an arduous task. But is both a bold and achievable strategy, if you follow through with an equally well executed set of tactics, and your personal goal is worthwhile.

You have to identify the people who can swim, and establish their individual capacity. You have to involve them in your goal. You have to motivate them to swim for you. And you then have to reward them for their effort, so that they may choose to help you in the future.

You can only do this if you truly are aware of what each person is seeking for themselves, and clearly demonstrate how by helping you, they will in turn, be helping themselves.

And any short-changing on your behalf will diminish their capacity to succeed for you, so in cheating them, you ultimately cheat yourself. Nothing sours quicker the taste of victory than the image of a cheat.

This is true of anything you choose to do in life. When you cut corners, take the easy way out, short change someone, hold something back by not giving your all, you effectively poison your intellect. The scars on your soul are testimony to this, and the single most damning limitation you can place on the development of your personal power is to attempt to lie or cheat your way to success.

It can never happen. The purity of your soul determines the amount of energy available to be used by you, in anything you do. And your soul has a God-given ability to determine what you will be capable of. You cannot lie to it. You cannot cheat it. You cannot fool it.

Just as if you attempted to swim between the short sides to achieve your great distance, you effectively are making your task all that much the harder, because you suddenly have three or four times as many turns to make, robbing you of the vital energy needed to complete the swim.

You will wear yourself out doing the least important thing in the process of achieving your goals - changing direction.

People learn what they want to learn, when they want to learn it. People do things best, when they do things they want to do, when they want to do them. In other words, when there is a heavily internalised desire to learn or do something for "self", it will become the most powerful motivating force in the person with whom you are establishing a relationship.

If it is not already obvious in their bearing, character, or outward stance, then this is what you need to stimulate in everyone you need to swim for you.

You need them to swim for you, but for their reasons. They must understand that they are helping you to achieve your goal, but that they are doing it so that they will achieve some of their goals. And you must become the perfect mirror - only showing them pure, positive, good images, that will enable them to achieve for you (and therefore achieve for themselves) what it is you want of them, in the most efficient manner possible.

Efficiency is a bitter word. It can be charming, but it usually dredges up images of tough black-suited people cracking whips and carrying large stopwatches. But it is a very necessary concept, because like swimming between the short sides, inefficiency is an energy draining, mind numbing, soul destroying activity that drags you down. Inefficiency is the blackest of all the attitudinal cancers, infecting and corroding all around it. It catches on like wildfire, moving from person to person faster than a speeding bullet.

Simply put, efficiency (competency, effectiveness, practicality, and sensibility) is doing something once, well, and with the minimum of fuss and expended energy. When you are in this mode, all around you adopt the same mindset. It's like a cooling wind on a hot day, that suddenly brings relief - you feel better, you feel energised, and you feel more powerful just for being exposed to it.

When you execute your goals in an efficient manner, you are paying the greatest compliment possible to those people you have chosen to help you achieve your goal. Because by conserving your energy, and minimising the trauma, you are conserving their energy, and maximising their respect for you and your goals.

No one likes to think that they are wasting their time or energy, because both are precious commodities.

If you stop and think about all the people you regard as role models, or people whom you look up to, it will become apparent that part of their attraction is their calmness, their organised manner, their considerate nature, and their engaging personalities.

For you to be a role model to those around you whom you need to influence and motivate, you also need these qualities.

There is one other quality you should seek in others - because you believe in it yourself - and that is the definite mantle of excellence.

The people you choose to swim for you must be the very best there are, under the circumstances. Just as a chain is weakened by a faulty link, so is overall performance degraded by a poor effort or intent. The quality of what you achieve will always only be as good as the lowest common denominator is capable of executing.

It is of little value to you or your people to achieve the goal, but lose your desire in the process. The attainment of your objective should be the point at which you realise your maximum flux of personal power, not suffer the draining experience of a negative victory.

There are many different sizes and shapes of swimming pool, and all have to be approached cautiously, one at a time, for their lessons in life. And while your ambition to swim 10 k's in each may remain the same, with as great an intensity as your original goal, the manner in which you do it will have to change dramatically, depending on the physical qualities of each pool.

This point may seem terribly simple, and obvious. But it is usually the obvious that escapes most people. Some would approach an ornamental kidney-shaped pool, and instantly decide that it isn't even worth the effort to try to swim 10 kilometres. Just the shape of the pool, the assumed degree of difficulty, and the lack of genuine desire is enough to stall them in their tracks, denying them the opportunity of ever achieving their goals.

The person who wants wealth, prosperity, success and personal power sees the kidney-shaped pool quite differently.

He sizes it up, measures it out, tests the water with his toe, confirms the deeps and shallows, and sometimes, if he is highly committed to achieving his goals, shucks off his clothes, and goes for a test swim. The whole time, he is regarding the shape and nature of the pool as a challenge that must be met in the most efficient way. Not a barrier or obstacle, but a test of his will-power, a challenge to his comfort zone.

And by internalising his experience in working out the strategy he must employ to achieve his objective, he is firming up his resolve, giving life to his vision, and empowering his intellect to assist in arriving at excellent conclusions. These positive attributes will shine from his eyes as he tells his people what it is they must do.

And because he believes, so will they, and with an intensity that exactly matches his. In effect, they have become a mirror of his goal, the physical manifestation of his achievement. He has found the keys to their success, and in the process of unlocking their power, he will achieve his goal.

Every swimming pool in life has to be swum, at one time or another. You cannot avoid your responsibilities, just as you cannot deny your destiny.

What you can do, is face your future with a pure soul, and engage those around you to force-multiply your talent. Learn to help people find their source of personal power, and in the process, learn to use their skills to help you find yours.

# THE ISLAND OF "I"

This is where you find out
just how important a person
you really are!

There's no one in the whole world more important than you! Keep this in mind as you read the next chapter, and believe it, because it's true.

Instinctively, you may poohah this notion, and if that's your reaction, then consider this.

Why should anyone allocate any values to you, if you are not prepared to allocate some to yourself?

And why should someone else's opinion be higher, or better, than the opinion you hold of yourself?

The answers to this conundrum lie within the confines of your own self-confidence and self-esteem, so if you are unable to immediately and without question accept that you are the key to your Universe, then be patient, and read on.

The development of personal power relies heavily on how you perceive yourself, not only in the isolation of self-examination, but in the competitive environment of the social structure within which we all live.

Everything has a beginning, a middle, and an end. Everything in life has a start, a middle, and a finish. You are born, you live out your life, then you die.

Many of us believe that what you do with your life between birth and death, the "middle", is what "it" - life - is all about.

In truth, it's not what you do that counts, it's how well you try to do it!

It's your performance and attitude that gives you the buzz, not the achievement.

Even though you may stand on the ultimate level of success, flushed with the pride of recognition, it is not the instant of reward or acknowledgment that is the pay-off. Your true worth is the sum total of all your experiences, and long after the milling crowd has forgotten who you are, and what you did, you will still have the internalised values you acquired through your diligence and effort in getting to your goal.

Understanding is exactly the same - first you come to grips with the fact that you don't know what it is you need to know (to understand), then you go about learning all the facts and things you need, and then, finally, you understand.

But it's the process of learning where everything good takes place, and you measure your achievement by what you do with this new understanding. I'll say that again - "you measure your achievement by what you do with this new understanding" - not by what the understanding is.

Personal power grows as you do, like a slow burning fuse heading for a gigantic bomb.

You are reading this book, making value judgements as you go, absorbing some points, and selectively filtering out others. You don't even necessarily have to think about it, you just do it. But you don't consider the ability to "read" as any great feat, because you remember the fun and enjoyment you had (and still get) from the process of reading, not the fact that you can read.

Being able to read gives you limitless options in the possible execution of your reading skills. But if you don't use them, then your ability is worthless.

No winner's medal for learning to read, but plenty of gold medals for using your reading ability to advance your intellect.

The same goes for stretching your comprehension, and enhancing your attitude.

All of which will help you to develop your personal power.

This is what getting new, pure understanding is all about.

If, at the end of the process, you perceive little or no worth for your new understanding, then the understanding you have gained is of little value. But you have achieved a great deal by going through the process of learning - what we call the "middle effort" - and that in itself is valuable, and shouldn't be discounted out of hand.

And it is this "middle" from where you derive the most benefit, even if you do not achieve your original goal - of getting a new understanding, that you could do something with.

Sounds like double Dutch, doesn't it?

But what it comes down to is as simple as this.

It's what you do with your life that counts, not what you may or may not collect on the way.. Very few of us ever come to truly understand this, and it is perhaps the biggest single problem we all face in growing our personal power to the limits.

Constantly you are faced with the public pressure and perception that you should perform or try to attain standards set by others.

But as we have just discovered, the only values you need strive for are your own, and not someone else's.

Because, throughout life, there is only the one absolute apart from the fact that one day you will die - and that is the literal truth. Everything else is a derivation, an interpretation, an extrapolation, a perception, or a figment of someone's imagination.

And the literal truth about you, is that you are the only one who can be "you".

No one else can, no matter how hard they may try.

You are the only one with your fingerprints.

The only one with your special mix of DNA, the sub-molecular biogenetic building blocks that make us each the unique, individual person that we are.

You determine who you will be.

You determine what you will be.

You determine how you will be
perceived by others.

You determine how you will be judged
by others.

You determine how you will be valued
by others.

You determine how fast or slow you
will be - whatever it is you are to
be.

And in the final analysis, you are the only one who can determine how successful you are at whatever it is that you have become, or will become in the future, or choose to do.

You will determine how much personal power you develop, and how you use your personal power. No one else can do it for you, even if they wanted to.

Now you see why "you" are so important
- to you!

A lot of every day, you are going to be doing things that are vitally important to you, and your development as a wholesome, integrated personality, but not necessarily as important or vital to those around you.

You have to get "you" right, before anyone else can follow. And that means you have to be a little selfish, examining everything from your perspective, to discover what new and beneficial kernels of wisdom and understanding are there for the taking.

It's this constant need to internalise the exterior process that sometimes gets you into trouble with the people around you, even though what you are doing is right, and vital to you.

They don't understand what you are doing. They don't understand why, and they don't understand how important it is to you. And because they are not as aware of the process as you are, they attempt to pollute your mind and your value system with heaps of scorn and selfish criticism, which, if you're weak in any area, will work itself into your psyche and become destructive, lessening your personal power.

It is a natural predatory tendency of the human animal to attack someone weaker than themselves, not just to prove how clever or strong they are, but also to remind you that they know you're weak.

And it is an established fact (but not necessarily a literal truth) that the polluted garbage we take into our psyches from other people is the most damaging of all, right next to the polluted garbage we invent for ourselves!

The simple solution? Develop your own value system, decide on your own self-worth, and confidently radiate your newly professed self-image. And be prepared to upset a few people with your positive stance, because just as the predators like to suborn the weak with their power, they are equally uncomfortable with any display of confidence by you.

Let no one person ever put you down for their reasons, and never accept a reflected value less than that which you set for yourself.

After all, you are the only person who can be you, so why should you?

Your personal power depends on you, remember.

There are always two choices. There's "YES", there's "NO", and then there's all the other stuff between a "YES" and a "NO". You can choose to decide "YES" or "NO", (one choice) or you can wallow around in the grey areas of life, bouncing from pillar to post, lost in confusion, rationalisation, and indecision. (The other, second choice).

35

A lot of every precious day is spent in this most damning area of grey. Sometimes you even enjoy it, failing to understand that every second spent in indecision is taking precious lifetime from you, with absolutely no return!

If you do nothing else with this Handbook of Personal Power, take this to heart - do not wallow between "YES" and "NO".

If you cannot make a "YES", then make a "NO", and start the understanding process to find out and learn what you need to make the "YES". It's that simple. All you have to do is decide to do something, and everything will fall into place.

There's the tried and tested One-Five-Ten rule, origin unknown, that you can fall back on if nothing else comes to mind. It will help you overcome indecision and that most dreaded state, inertia.

One means that if you do just something that's 1% positive in the general direction you think the solution to the problem might lay, then something will happen that will head you towards the answer. The idea here is that just by doing something, rather than nothing, you get your creative juices flowing, and open up the fertile world of limitless possibilities.

The value Five is a little bit more focussed - you're looking for a 5% input of energy, streamed towards the probable solution, and experience tells us that you can expect a high probability of success in solving the problem.

By now you've guessed that the Ten value demands a whole 10% of focussed energy, directed exclusively at resolving the issues. There is little doubt that 10% of your best effort can solve practically any problem, given that some of us cruise along in life at never more than an estimated 3% of our capacity at any given time!

Every person is an Island, standing alone in a sea of choices, and humankind is the only animal on Earth that has the power to choose. Let a dog loose in a paddock, and you'll get a lot of holes. Let you loose in a paddock, and you'll get everything from a Shopping Centre to a Space Port, with all the drama in between.

Now, everyone knows this, yet very few ever make the most important choice of all - to do something with their lives. It's almost as if developing your personal power is too hard. The very fact that you are reading this Handbook of Personal Power suggests that you are not someone blighted with this deadly, mind-numbing short-sightedness.

You want to empower your intellect, and develop your personal power to its fullest capacity.

The simple problem seems to be that it takes some energy to make a difference, and it is all too easy to sit back and watch life go by in glorious colour, with stereophonic sound, on a high-definition television set, than it is to participate.

But as you know only too well, you get back out of life what you put into it.

Not a penny more, not a penny less.

Humankind (yes, you) is the only animal on Earth that has the ability to create, to dream, to speculate, to think laterally, and to combine the elements into purpose-designed artefacts. You don't see a lot of cows living in high-rise apartments, or driving expensive cars to chrome and glass towering city buildings.

If it is okay to accept that we are the predominant culture on the surface of the earth, and that it is our destiny to evolve from our humble beginnings into a futuristic society, then why is it not so okay to stand on your own two feet, and be counted for the values you hold dear to your own heart? And develop your personal power as God meant you to do?

Man is the quintessential thinker, dreamer, creator, designer, builder, constructor, motivator, and doer.

In fact, throughout all history, in every field of human endeavour, with but one exception, nothing has ever been achieved in this world until a man or a woman has done something!

Things do not happen by themselves. You make them happen, or they simply do not take place.

If you cannot make a "YES", then make a "NO", and get on with solving the problem that is preventing you from making a "YES." The key issue is to get on with making something happen, and not sitting back in a blue fugue waiting for a miracle!

Science would have us believe that miracles don't really happen, and even if they are wrong, it is better to do something under your control than be under the control of others.

Personal power is personal. It is yours, and yours alone. You can share the benefits, but you cannot share the power. Only what you do with it.

What the mind can conceive, man can do. I'm sure someone has told you this before. And it's true. Once something has been thought about, it's just a matter of time and resources before it's done, whatever it is.

Look at just one simple, yet humanly enduring example.

In the fourteenth century, just over five hundred years ago, a very clever man dreamed up the concept of manned flight, sitting on a cold, cobblestone floor. From his lofty perch near the top of a buttressed tower, which was usually pressed into service to repel nasty aggressors with bows and arrows, he watched an eagle soar overhead, cutting the sun into shadow and light. It so inspired him he dreamed of being up there, floating on the warm afternoon breeze, peering down at the rich green meadow below. He framed a wild, bizarre idea in his capricious mind, thought about it for a whole day, then sketched it out with a handmade quill, onto a piece of tanned animal hide.

It took another three hundred years for mankind to develop the technology that enabled yet another clever man to actually build this "flying device", and get it to work. He drew up his idea with the handmade prototype of the fountain pen, using a distilled black substance that would later become known as "Indian Ink", in free-flowing broad strokes that gracefully covered five sheets of quality French parchment paper.

The drawings were of a simple hot-air balloon, made out of stitched hand-worked animal skins, amazingly similar to the hide the original drawings had been made on three hundred years before.

Those primitive sketches showed a languorous envelope being filled by the heat from a peat fire, stoked by a terrified blacksmith. The contraption that eventually flew, carrying its creator up some hundreds of feet into the cold mountain air, changing for all time how we would move about our planet, looked like a colourful child's toy that had been made too large!

Just a scant two hundred years later, men have walked on the Moon, sent satellites far out into space to explore the Universe, and routinely use small electronic devices that hold more information and distilled wisdom in one tiny microchip, than existed in the whole of the known world at the time our would-be flier defied all the odds to rise gracefully above his peers.

So what is the secret to all this?

You are!

The Island of "I", the home of your personal power.

Because everything ever achieved by mankind started with a single person, just like you.

And that's why it is so important that you get you right.

If you accept that the only person you have any real control over is you, then it is up to you to get you in the finest working order possible.

You cannot hope to influence anyone else unless you are in your strongest, purest, most powerful mental condition. And that state of activity starts, and centres on, your self-image.

Bad self-image, weak external perception.

Pure self-image (notice the word "pure", not "perfect"), strong external perception.

You will never be perfect, at least not on the outside, and certainly not perceived as such by someone else, but this is better explained in the chapter titled "The Power of "P"".

Stop and think about this for a minute.

Companies don't do things, people do.

Motor cars don't go Sunday driving along the beach road, people do.

Apartment blocks and fine houses don't give character to a neighbourhood, the people who design them, decorate them, live in them, and see them for what they really are, do.

The most sophisticated and expensive electronic device is useless, and serves no purpose, unless it is doing the bidding of a person.

The most incredibly efficient shopping plaza with all its attendant regalia of brightly lit malls, colourful shop fronts, enticing signs, and demanding merchandise is dormant and mute, useless in the early morning light, unless, to the melodious clank and clatter of waking commerce, you bring it to life with your presence.

You may not see yourself as the master of your Universe, but you should, and you are, every time you choose to exert your influence, and use your personal power. Because you were born, (and it is your birthright to be a complete, unique, experiential human being, capable of magnificent thoughts and actions), you at least owe it to yourself to reach your potential, or die trying.

The only limitations placed on you are those you place on yourself - or worse, allow others to place on you. It's very much like the pressure that drives you to take actions you feel uncomfortable about.

You perceive that the pressure is being applied by some-one (or some situation) in such a way that you have no alternative but to respond, and do something. The truth is, the pressure may be being applied, but it is your acceptance of the pressure that creates the problem for you, not the other person, or the situation, that seems to be applying the pressure.

If you choose not to respond to the pressure, it will diminish! It may not completely go away, but it will lessen in its intensity.

Let's look at it piece by piece.

If the pressure being applied is from another person, by refusing to let yourself be affected by the pressure, you lessen that person's ability to influence you. By standing firm, self-contained and in control, you empower your intellect, your reflexes, and free up the total sum of all that you have learned and experienced in life, expressly for the purpose of dealing with the problem.

You bring the mighty force of your personal power to bear on the problem.

If the pressure is being applied by your perception of a physical occurrence - a car crash, a fire, a threat of some kind, or a situation that seems out of your control, by accepting the pressure unchallenged you fuel your "fight or flight" reflex, depriving you of your fullest abilities to think, observe, plan, and act.

You are, in fact, achieving the exact opposite of what you need - you are depowering your intellect, and robbing yourself of your personal power.

Now it is extremely hard to agree with this if you are the one being threatened by the speeding train, as it roars down on you, bound hand and foot to the rails!

But ask yourself this one question. What was it that you did in the first place to get yourself into such a dire situation?

Without a single doubt, somewhere way back at the start, or soon after, you accepted someone else's pressure, or the assumed or perceived pressure from an untenable situation.

It's exactly the same as the office without a door, with a big sign posted to its frame - "As you can clearly see for yourself, this door is always open, unless you perceive it to be shut!"

Every worthwhile door in life is always open, should you choose to see it that way. On the other hand, if you perceive it to be shut, why, then, it is, as surely as if it had massive steel bars running across it from top to bottom.

It's how you view the things in life that determines how and when they can affect you.

Smile, and the whole world smiles with you. (Where have you heard that before?)

It doesn't matter who you are, or where you were born, how rich or poor your parents were, how much schooling you got, or what you think you should or shouldn't be capable of, you will never really know what an incredible life you can have unless you try.

And that means that you must be aware, you must seek, you must question, you must try different things, you must read and strive for new understanding, and then you must take risks, in trying to implement what you have learnt.

And you can never willingly accept pressure from another person, of from a situation. You must be in control, and able to use your full facilities, to bring the awesome weight of your experience, wisdom, and understanding to the problem.

The full might of your personal power!

Making mistakes is a very human attribute, because no one person is perfect.

You have never met someone who is, and you never will. You have met many who say they are, act like they are, and even believe they are. But I bet you saw right through them, and perhaps even brought their delusion to their attention.

Even if you didn't get your lights punched out, then it's a fair guess that they are not a friend of yours at this time.

You see, the concept of perfection is a spiritual one, and is truly not obtainable in the physical sense. When was the last time you saw or heard of a perfect motor car? Or a toaster? Or a lawn-mower? Or even a perfect computer?

Perfection, by definition, "completion; making perfect; full development; faultlessness;" is not an achievable thing as far as human beings are concerned, and that goes for anything we do in this Universe.

Those of you who are deeply religious will recognise this statement in the context of the teachings of your Church, Guru, Master, Rabbi, Deacon or Spiritual Leader. The Bible, Koran, Myan Scrolls, Dead Sea Scrolls, I'Ching, and every other Guide Book you read spells this concept out in exquisite detail, so we won't belabour the point here. It is sufficient for you to under-stand this secret - don't kill yourself trying for perfection, unless you are striving for spiritual wholeness.

And even then, make damn sure you know exactly what you are doing beforehand!

However, one vital tip. Always give "permission" to those around you to make mistakes, because if you don't, you will be denying them their right to experiment and be human. Just because you seek perfection within yourself, is no reason to seek it in others.

Just as it is your right to seek your answers as you choose, so it is everyone else's right to seek or not seek their answers, as they choose.

And make their own mistakes, if that's what it takes for them to achieve their understanding, in their own time.

And develop their personal power for their benefit.

The best you can hope for on this Earth is achieving the perfect State of Grace, or Inner Stance. This issue is discussed in detail in the Chapter titled, "The Sealed Section Part Three - Getting right to the Heart of the Matter", in Part 2. See you there soon.

In the meantime, you must learn to make a choice based on real things, real situations, real information, and real perceptions, and not on wishful thinking.

And you must choose a "YES" or a "NO", and not wallow in self-delusion, allowing confusion and indecision to rob you of your personal power.

Now there's a interesting word.

Power!

Every person has it, but uses it to varying degrees. What makes you the most uncomfortable is someone exerting their power over you, dominating you and not allowing you to be yourself.

So turn the page, and you'll quickly get a helpful tip or two to straighten out that situation, we guarantee it!

And then personal power will be yours, and yours alone.

As it was always meant to be.

# THE POWER OF "P"

This might feel like
you're about to chew
on a dictionary,
but hang in there,
the "P" words are where
your personal power comes from.

The vertical "P".

No one likes to be dominated by another person, chastised for poor performance, or taken for granted by their peers. Just as you can never win an argument, because it is an emotional event, and not rational, you can never hope to impress someone who counts in your life with external values.

You may well make an impression, and it might even be a good one, but the gloss will soon wear off as the discussion or relationship develops, because what you say and do will be at odds with how you look.

How you feel is another matter.

"Clothes maketh the Man" is an old saying, and a false one. Clothes maketh the outside of the Man, giving you a certain appearance, which may generate a certain bearing in your external stance. What happens is that the process of getting, then putting on, a new dress or exquisitely cut new suit pumps you up emotionally, charges your ego with false power symbols, and allows you to strut your stuff for all to see.

But an emotional fix is a purely horizontal experience, and as the dress or suit become worn with age, so does their ability to pump you up.

A horizontal experience is one that is flat, only able to generate a short term boost, that often is just a repeat of the same old thing, but perhaps in a different form.

Now, there's nothing wrong with a short term emotional ego fix, so long as you recognise it for what it is, and don't become seduced by it. Anything that's external, sucked in emotionally, or built on a false, short term premise, is potentially misleading, and harmful.

Why? Because it's all too easy to accept an abnormal situation as reality, and get drunk on the temporary thrill and power surge of external reinforcement. Trouble is, the hangover from an ego drunk destroys your self-image, depreciates your self-worth, and robs you of your rightful personal power.

You can't fool the real you, no matter how hard you might try.

An internalised, or vertical experience, one that is taken inside to your very soul, lives on forever, and can provide endless stimulation and joy. Holding a newborn baby for the first time, discovering you are in love, recognising the intrinsic value of true craftsmanship, are all examples of this most necessary type of experience.

The thrill and power that surges from doing new things, with new energy, can light up the dullest life!

Just as mankind is the only animal given the ability to choose, so is mankind the only species given the ability to differentiate between a horizontal and a vertical experience.

You have often heard people lust after all that is "new", or different. Who can resist the seductive smell that wafts delicately out of the interior of a new car? Or the super bullet-proof feeling of putting on a new, expensive dress or suit for the first time?

But no matter how new something may be, no matter how seductive its call, until you internalise the smell, the look, the touch, the feel, the warmth or the chill, and hear the crackle of the starch and the rip of the zipper, you will only enjoy your new experience but once, over and over again. (That's the danger of the horizontal.)

The majesty of a vertical experience is that it stays with you forever, adding to your total fund of experiences and knowledge. And every time you add to the experience, it gets all the more powerful, to the point where you can actually generate the feelings and the smells and the crackles in your own mind, without actually seeing the new object!

Visualisation is dealt with in some detail in The Sealed Section Part Two titled - "Mind over Matter". Worst case, you will find all that you need to better understand what a vertical experience is all about, and how it can empower you in your everyday life.

True Power comes from within, not from without, and is a manifestation of the purity of your soul, not a measure of your intellect or physical strength. One of the greatest scientists of our time lives in a shrunken, dyslexic body, and communicates with a stick clenched between dribbling teeth. But one look into his eyes, one quick snapshot of his soul, and the awesome power within him attacks you like a laser beam.

True power comes from recognising who a person is, not what they are, or might become. The simple cause of the modern disease of "opting out" is people's inability to cope with who they really are. They have strived so long, worked so hard, learned so much, yet inside they are hollow, empty, unfulfilled, and hurting. Simply because they concentrated on the horizontal experiences, gobbling them up like PACMAN, only to find that the feeling of achievement passed with the night, leaving precious little residue.

Look what happens to Olympians when they fail to take a Gold medal - the ordinary ones (lost in the grey void of the horizontal experience) fall down as losers, but the extraordinary ones shine with the glow of victory, because they recognise that the process of getting to the Olympics is the true achievement, the Gold medal only a short-lasting form of external measurement.

Of course they wanted to win Gold, and of course they are disappointed at not achieving their ambition. But because the "win" was but one small part of the process, and not the inglorious end, they are able to refocus themselves and not squander the emotional and physical achievement that has been derived through years of sacrifice and hard training.

Every elite athlete knows that practice doesn't make perfect, as most people would have you believe. Perfect practice makes perfect. The trouble with life is that all too often we are waylaid or misled by something someone says they know, or professes to know, better than we do. Or even worse, something we read and only partially understand, but try to operate on anyway.

We all too often run off fully charged only to discover that the path of our well-meaning effort leads to a dead end.

Well, now's the perfect time to take control of your life, and do away with all the misconceptions and half-truths that creep around us like so much choking pollution. Now is the time to recognise the frighteningly short value in the horizontal experience.

Now is the time to learn about the Power within you, just waiting to be tapped, a power all to do with towering vertical experiences. The simple, but awesome Power of the mighty "P" words.

The two "P" words that sting.

Most people are scared about pain, but we all know that no pain, no gain. There's no such thing as a free lunch. You get nothing for nothing. You only get out of life what you put into it, and the more you put in, the greater the return. So if it hurts sometimes when you are trying hard to do or learn something, that's good. But don't feel good about the pain, feel good about the gain! Remember, it's the process that you learn the most from, not the achievement.

Pain can also be a sign that you are using the wrong parts of your intellect or body to attempt the task with. If you are feeling decidedly uncomfortable mentally, then it's a good bet that you are trying to wade through confusion or deceit.

Pain is usually a physical signal that you are close to maxing out, reaching for a new level of physical capability and performance. And like anything physical, it can easily be controlled by discipline and training, and a positive mental attitude towards the task at hand. This is called "process". Remember, you only do well the things in life you want to do, so when you choose to do something, go for it.

It is this focus on energy and achievement that enables you to motivate yourself towards your goal, so always take the time to experience and enjoy the process of getting there. Many seconds make a minute, and sixty minutes make an hour. Take one second, or one minute away, and you have everything else but an hour.

And it is precisely because time passes by this point but once, that you should savour every split second, taste every minute, and revel in every hour you are given until the day you die. If you don't, you'll pass on feeling cheated of something you were vaguely aware of, but never quite able to put your finger on.

A full and invigorating dynamic life!

And the fullest use of your greatest asset - your personal power.

The perfect "P" within.

Everyone you meet lusts after a place called Paradise, but very few, if any one, can specifically describe this mystical place. It seems to vary from person to person, like a fast moving cloud. Yet they are all very positive that they seek it, and believe it to be better that where they are now. Paradise means "A garden of Eden; Heaven; A State of supreme bliss", so it is easy to guess what they really mean when they say they seek it.

They are looking for a way out of their present predicament - whatever that may be at the time, and they are always searching for something that they believe is being denied to them, but should be rightfully theirs.

Many Religions and their Sages would have us believe that we have to die in a State of Grace to go to Paradise, where God or some other Sentient Being is patiently waiting for the pleasure of our company.

Others would have us believe that you earn your ticks in the "Book of Life" as you go, and your entry to Paradise is dependent on having accumulated enough to pass through the Pearly Gates when you time has come.

This may or may not be true - this is up to you to determine - but what is true is that from the time of your birth, you have Paradise within you at all times. It's always there, just waiting for you to visit.

Paradise is "A garden of Eden; Heaven; A State of supreme bliss".

There's a marvellous old poem that is said to have made the rounds about five thousand years ago, in the Middle East where Babylon is thought to have been sited. It goes something like this, with no apology for the imperfect and somewhat liberal translation of the original Gortighern Script.

> "The rim of the wheel,
> it is made of steel,
> And the spokes
> that join it
> are of solid oak.
> But I know, as you do,
> That the mighty

brass hub
Is all but useless,
Unless the hole
in the middle
is not broke."

The mystics and scholars of ancient times had a very simplistic philosophy. They studied and viewed the known Universe in minute detail, then promptly cast everything into one of but two acceptable baskets of knowledge.

The first basket held the plausible, or that which was able to be explained to the satisfaction of the many, without causing the sudden death by stoning of the scholar doing the explaining. The second held everything implausible, or that which could not be easily explained using the signs and symbols of the physical Universe, and consequently demanded the label of "magic", "possessed by demons", or "spiritual".

Suffice to say that naked fear abounded in the presence the second basket, which from time to time was filled to the brim with wonder and unexplored mystery, drawing scholars to it like a flame draws moths.

It is said that the scholars that visited this second basket became very creative in the way they went about unravelling the seemingly implausible secrets of the Universe, taking care to have a sufficiency of proof before letting anyone else view their work. This tended to slow the natural process of discovery down somewhat, and might explain why the middle ages took so long to pass!

But by paying careful attention to the detail of their torrid existence, the scholars were able to slowly advance the knowledge of mankind, developing a wisdom far greater than the one we seem to have so casually adopted in this modern age of super-computers and spaceships.

Unlike now, nothing was taken for granted, and it was always assumed that everything in life had a purpose, if only it could be divined. And that it was mankind's responsibility to discover these universal secrets.

Their starting point on every voyage of discovery was that that which stood before them was no more than a temporary barrier between knowledge and mystery, put there by God to encourage them to greater wisdom, gained in the solving of the riddle.

They viewed the final uncovering, the reveal, the peeling back of the secrets of life like attacking so many layers of an onion skin. They patiently peeled each layer, one layer at a time, savouring the revelations and incredible discoveries they made on their specific journeys. The final result they presented to the world, but the knowledge and the experience they collected on the way they kept to themselves, fuelling their intellect, and swelling their personal power..

They discovered, for instance, that no matter how large a wheel, no matter how magnificent the construction, and no matter how noble the ultimate purpose, it's what was in the middle of the massive wheel that gives it its life.

A hole full of nothing!

Now, imagine for a minute, trying to explain that to a Saturday morning crowd at the market, five thousand years ago!

Until an axle was placed in the hole, the massive wheel could never fulfil its destiny. It could be used for many other things, what at best only added up to a rationalisation of its function, but never for its primary role until the little hole in the middle was filled with the right stuff!

What's in the middle of us all? What fills your core, your central "hole" through which the axle of life passes second by second?

Paradise is. "A garden of Eden. Heaven. A State of Bliss." Peace. Perspective. Perception. Potential. Personality. Power!

And a thousand other powerful "P" words, all just waiting to be visited. And you can prove it to the most virulent sceptic. But first, you have to learn (if you don't already know) how to get into your very own paradise any time you choose.

This is not a book about Meditation, it's a Handbook of Personal Power. But if you want to discover the majesty and beauty of your own Garden of Eden, your own personal State of Bliss, your very own Heaven on Earth, then go to the Chapter titled, "Unlocking the Secret of the Deep of the Soul". (The Handbook of Personal Power, Part 2.)

Believe it when it's said that Paradise is within us all, available now, just for the visiting, and it's the place where all your real personal power comes from, so get acquainted real soon.

Think about yourself as a scholar of old, possessing many secrets, but able to only share a few, lest you confuse your audience. Peel back the onion skin, one layer at a time, and savour the revelation of discovery as you learn all that is good about yourself.

Look inwards, not out, and start to appreciate the quiet, reflective moments that occur from time to time, and taste them for their worth. They are a path to your Paradise, just waiting to be used.

And Paradise is the battery which enables your personal power to flourish, and grow.

When you centre your focus, you gain a peace and tranquillity that is all empowering, and most often defies description. Your whole being seems to float in a sea of calm, and your awareness is heightened to the point where you find yourself solving amazingly difficult problems with alarming ease. You gain a new perspective about your role and place in the Universe, and you allow your mind and your body to heal and draw closer to each other, integrating your personality.

What do you find when you peel back the final layer of the onion? What is the vital core of a tennis ball? Which part of a water tank is the most valuable?

Within the onion, nothing.

The inside of a tennis ball is composed of air, or empty space.

And that space of nothingness which is contained by the walls of the tank is what the tank exists for!

The "hole" in the middle of us all, through which we pass on our journey of life.

Anyone who would, through scorn or ridicule, attempt to prevent you from discovering this secret about yourself, deserves your best smile, and tolerance. Naked fear still abounds around that second basket, the one filled with the unpalatable. And a deep distrust of the unknown still drives an ungodly proportion of the world along the path of ignoble ignorance.

But no so you, especially now, that you are on the vertical path to develop your personal power.

The bewildering "P".

Our lives are full of paradox - contradictions abound, inconsistency is the norm, and it's almost incongruous to expect anything better. But there's Power in paradox, if you take the time to understand it. A paradox is no more than a person, a thing, or a statement that apparently conflicts with your preconceived notions of what is reasonable, correct, or possible. What is palatable. The key words - apparently conflicts with your preconceptions - say it all.

By understanding that your confusion stems from brain lock - that dreaded self-inflicted state of inertia, where you deprive yourself of your power at the time you most need it - you give yourself the best fighting chance to resolve the conflict of perception verses apparent fact. It's a strange observation, but it appears that facts change little in their lifetime, but our perceptions alter constantly. It seems to depend on our awareness, our mood, our state of fitness, our mental alertness, and on the level of our genuine desire to understand, rather than just take the things around us for granted.

Scientists have an adequate description of the phenomenon, in that they relate Paradox as that "which an observer, standing in the centre of his Universe, discovers to be two or more things that apparently conflict, resulting in the attitude that both cannot possibly be true at the same time."

This enigmatic state occurs frequently in the physical world, and can only be resolved by tedious observation, experimentation, and study. But when it occurs in your mind, it is a simple thing to deal with.

You just back off a pace, realise that your perception is at odds with the facts, and determine to resolve the issue. Establish what is what, accept the reasonable, and question the unreasonable. And never take anything at face value.

The two baskets of knowledge still exist today, and their purpose is still the same. One allows easy acceptance of a deluge of known things, the other a passive, non-threatening way to deal with the unknown. A paradox is simply something that seems to cross or link some of the contents of the two baskets, and to be resolved, all you need do is discover which basket it comes from, which basket it belongs in, and what you have to do to put it safely away where it belongs.

And if that seems paradoxical, spend some quiet time thinking about the consequences if you don't!

The "T" and "D" of "P".

Don't be limited by what you think you know. It's an easy trap for young players, and an often used refuge from the pain of truth. You know that there's no gain without some degree of pain, no matter how small. Real personal power comes from real understanding, and real work, not from preconceptions or self-delusion, so take the time to really find out exactly what's what with your world.

Just as you cannot see through someone else's eyes, they cannot clearly see through yours. To see your world, you must use your eyes, and experience your learning and understanding, for yourself. Nothing worthwhile, other than well-meaning advice, comes second hand.

It is easy to assume things, and even easier to ignore truth. But where is the possible gain? A saving of effort? Life time spent somewhere else? You cheat only yourself, and lower your self-worth. Just as you are the only one who can determine your truth for you, so are you the only one who can do your real work for you.

And ultimately, you are the one who benefits.

The only real pressure that exists, is that which you place on yourself, so take all the time you need to search out the truth in life. In reality, that's what you are here for. To discover your truth for your life, empowering your soul to fulfil your destiny.

Pressure comes in many disguises, from demand and anxiety, all the way to frustration and exterior influence. But like a hosepipe with both a tap at one end, and a controllable outlet at the other, you always have two distinct ways to deal with perceived pressure.

You can shut it off at the source by refusing to accept it from another person or situation; or you can "tune" it to your advantage at the other end, by deciding how much, and in what form, you will accept the pressure you perceive is being placed on you.

Either way, all it takes is a conscious effort not to let it dominate you, and you will suddenly be empowered to deal with it, in any form it may strike you.

The downside of accepting pressure from others to per-form in certain ways, is that it is like a cancer, eating away at your confidence and your abilities. It is insidious, and it can be lethal.

Pressure, stress, confusion, and frustration can kill you, maim your brain, and destroy your personality. But it need not be so.

Just imagine the hosepipe, and either shut off the tap, or tune the nozzle to the required amount.

The inner "P".

It may be hard to accept at face value, but there are no worthwhile prizes for meandering through life other than those that you award yourself. You are the only person who can accu-rately assess how well you are performing at any given time, because you are the only one who has access to your soul. Everyone else is looking in from the outside, seeing only that which you choose to project as your physical manifestation of who and what you are at any given time.

To seek the rewards of others is a short term fix to stitch up an ego problem, caused by a lack of wholeness. When you hold up the mirror of life, what you see is what you get. But you can also see inside you, and you can see what your life is really all about.

To flush with the warm feeling of externalised positive reinforcement is only of value when you internalise the praise or support you have been offered, taking it to a new dimension. You clutch the strong positive feeling of a sense of achievement to your heart, and you fuel your soul. This internalising is what keeps you going from day to day, seeking your truths.

While graciously accepting the praise or confirmation of your achievement from others, always be aware that it is what you do with it that counts, not the praise itself. It's the process we learn from, not the achievement. You are the one who must award the prizes for your endeavours, and you are the only one who can accurately and honestly value and judge your performance.

And as you will discover, to do this you have to know who you are, and what you are, and accept yourself from within for all that you are and can be.

However, having said that, be advised that as most of the world around you is not as aware as you are, true praise is the most constructive reinforcement you can ever offer someone else. Nothing boosts self-confidence and self-worth faster than an ego charging honest compliment from someone respected.

The public "P".

You need to stir the beast of Pride, generating positive energy within yourself, and face the reality of your existence, whatever that may be. To be proud of something, you have to believe in its intrinsic worth and value, otherwise you simply fool yourself. You have to openly commit to it, overtly declaring your feelings for all to see.

And that's a very difficult and dangerous thing to do, because the moment you declare your intentions publicly, the razor sharp knife of prejudice comes out, heading for your back. (Or, if you live in some Countries, you could get stabbed in the front!)

But if you use Pride as your stimulant in everything you do, then it will only be the really impossible situation that defeats you, and even then, only temporarily. You can be proud of your best effort, and your best attitude. You can be proud of your achievements, and of conquering process. You can also be proud of your inner stance, and the way it affects those around you.

"Pride cometh before a fall". True, and certainly if you become lost in it, at the sacrifice of your true values. But if you use Pride as a means of setting self-standards, then you will never fail.

For how could you ever, knowingly, let yourself down?

It would be most unworthy of you, and it would rob you of your hard earned personal power.

The powerful "P".

You need to understand the incredible force of Patriotism, and stand tall amongst your peers, recognising that you may well make them feel decidedly uncomfortable with your naked display of pride and emotion. If you cannot feel proud about your Country, if you cannot shed a genuine tear at the playing of the national Anthem, and the raising of the Flag, then you should abandon you place, and go somewhere else, for you can never really feel proud about yourself.

Any measure of a lack of respect for something or some-one, no matter how small and seemingly insignificant, burdens you with a double measure of lack of self-respect. You intuitively know what is right, and your psyche punishes your soul when you are not true to yourself.

Man does not easily dwell on the fringe of life, it is not his purpose, so recognise this, and start developing a feel for the strength and sense of belonging a nationalistic stance can generate within you.

Your Country is a great one, brought to life with your intellect and physical presence.

Don't ever deny it, and don't ever turn your back on it.

You make its History, you create its Culture, and you determine its Future, if it is to have one.

Just as your personal power allows you to achieve all the goals you have set for yourself, so will it contribute to the growth of your Nation.

This awesome responsibility comes with Citizenship and Nationality, from the day your are born, or arrive, and can never be denied.

The primary "P".

This County is a boundless series of arid deserts, strolling mountains, furious seas, and a patchwork quilt of colour and intrigue. But it takes you to bring it to life, to add that extra dimension of colour and activity that gives it its unique culture.

For millions of years, this Country has been evolving slowly and deliberately, nudged here and there by fleeting traumatic and sometimes cataclysmic events. The dinosaurs have come and gone, seas have conquered and receded, and mountains have erupted only to be worn smooth by the irresistible passage of time.

Compared to this gigantic, unstoppable evolutionary process, the transient nature of the minuscule life-span of a single human being is but a mote in God's eye. But the years we are given us at Birth can be used to develop a harmony with our ever pulsing environment, and use our earth-sense to generate internal power.

This is not a "save the environment" speech. This is a "savour the environment" plea.

Feel the warmth of rich red earth running through your fingers. Smell the rain on a gum leaf. Absorb the rolling sound of thunder as you recharge your soul with the strident music from a naked flash of lightning. Take your shoes off, and let the moist mud and sand filter up between your toes as they talk to your feet.

Watch the waking birds with your ears on a crisp winter morning, and imagine what it would be like to walk across a moonbeam flickering on a placid ocean.

Just the simple process of absorbing the magic and majesty of the world around you charges you batteries - your Paradise - and causes your personal power to bloom and flower.

It is, after all, your world to enjoy for your four score years and ten. You owe it to yourself to seek and find your true relationship with your environment, that's why humankind was given the gift of the five senses. Use them, and use them well, because in finding your balance within your environment, your are finding your balance within yourself. And like all things dynamic, if you don't use your senses, they deteriorate in terms of sensitivity.

And personal power depends on stimulus, and renewable energy, so don't let any of your senses go slack, lest you deprive yourself of valuable experience.

Earth symbols are very powerful in our lives, but all too few people ever see the incredible potential of summoning them. Yet they govern our very existence, influence our every mood, and colour our every achievement. The primary "P" is one of the most powerful of all, yet, strangely, it is perhaps the least understood and used!

Our forefathers understood this far better than we do now, as the unstoppable march of technology seems to have desensitised us to our heritage. But like any Paradox, all it takes to reverse the trend is to recognise it, cast away the grey areas of indecision, and do something that brings music to your soul.

Earth music!

The inquisitive "P".

There's a lovely dichotomy in the endless debate between Art and Science - which is which, and what applies to each. Truth is, both apply and directly effect each other in the perpetual search for the answers to the mysteries of life, and in many ways this parallel debate reflects the development of your personality.

If you choose to be a "pioneer", always striving for understanding and enlightenment, breaking new ground, exploring the realm of possibilities, one day you will stand on the pinnacle of knowledge, and see it for what it is.

Your batteries (inner Paradise) will be constantly charged with vertical experiences that will stack up before you like a massive harbour bridge.

But no one person can ever hope to absorb everything available in the span of a single lifetime. There's simply too much knowledge to cope with. But wisdom can come cheaply, and with a simple change of attitude, you will see first-hand that you don't need to know everything to have a rich and long life, you only have to know yourself.

And the best knowledge comes from true discovery, true process, and true experience.

Wisdom (discipline, common or good sense, judgement, knowledge and philosophy) is simply the force you apply in the use of your personal power, enabling you to achieve your dreams without causing harm to those around you.

You need to exclusively live in the world of positive energy, making things possible because you want them to be, not necessarily because they are. You need to be praiseworthy in your endeavours, which simply means that what you choose to do is always worthwhile in real terms, and excellent in execution. Now excellence can be a well-worn standard, and rarely achieved in spite of the brouhaha that surrounds its use in modern day language.

But excellent also means "heavenly" and "precious", so take these meanings to heart, and ensure that everything you do, no matter how small, is executed "heavenly" because the action is "precious" to you.

Exquisite little touches of excellence delight, and light the path to Heaven. The Mystics of ancient years believed this, and over two thirds of the world has evolved with this simple philosophy as their principle guide.

The strongest nation on Earth is but a stage for the delicate skills of a Master, for who here can refuse an honest man, with honest skills, and honest endeavour?

The secondary "P".

Profound wisdom is not the exclusive domain of the well-educated. Profound wisdom is your right, and the right of all who choose to seek it. Knowing one small simple fact and being able to intelligently and excellently benefit from it provides the basis for profound wisdom. It is this "understanding" that sits comfortably within your core from where the personal power within you can be generated. It is your wisdom which determines how much power you have at any one given time. It is also your wisdom which determines how you use your power.

For when you have real power, and choose to use it, the only time it will work for you is when you exercise profound wisdom!

If you don't, then you may end up dominating someone, denigrating them in their own eyes, because of their lack of ability to cope with you. And as sure as night turns into day, your power will dissipate in the wind, leaving you unfulfilled and empty, angry and embarrassed, and afraid to face the mirror of life.

You can cheat everyone and anything for a short while, but you can never cheat your soul or who you really are, not even for a second. And the only time you don't have your power is when you know inside you that you don't deserve it, because its negative use is, or would be, destructive.

And we've already discovered that you are a builder, a creator, a dreamer, a thinker, a doer. All these attributes come to life when underpinned with your profound wisdom, and the strength of your intellect.

The bridging "P".

If you take the attitude of a protector, always careful to see to the welfare and well-being of your peers and those around you, then you will automatically limit your potential to hurt. It is impossible for you to hurt yourself if you are balanced and in harmony with all around you, just as it becomes impossible for you to hurt others.

Sensitivity is another human trait that is very much in danger of being swamped by all things electronic, simply because being sensitive takes great patience, great empathy, great warmth, great personal power, and a big heart. But by being sensitive to your environment, to those around you, and to your real needs, you attune your intellect and sharpen your awareness, allowing more of your internalised power to be used constructively.

Sensitivity is an attribute that is often frowned on by modern society, often mistaken for weakness or lack of power. In truth, the exact opposite it true. For you to be able to constantly allow your sensitivity to come to the fore, you must be self-confident, have a strong perspective of your role in life, and a high self-image.

And heaps and heaps of personal power.

Strange, isn't it, how the very things that make us strong, that make us what we are, that give us our real power to motor along in life with, sometimes appear to others as a weakness!

The tertiary "P".

If you take the role of a provider, then you will never allow yourself to take advantage of someone who has yet to find the "Gate of Wisdom". Rather, you will, at their request, help and guide them to find their own Paradise within themselves.

Remember people discover and learn what they want to learn, at their own rate, so offer support and guidance, don't push. Let them develop their own timetable, and allocate those resources they feel are necessary for the process of discovery. Don't judge them by their progress, but by their intent. And don't be hasty to celebrate a breakthrough, lest it be but the tip of the proverbial iceberg of knowledge and wisdom.

And should you find such a person, give them a copy of the Handbook of Personal Power, so that they too may find the Power of "P".

# YOU CAN'T FIGHT CITY HALL

The very first thing
we are taught by our parents
is that you can't
(and shouldn't) fight Authority.
Maybe they are right,
but then again ..

The real trick in life is to discover for yourself what you think is true, what is literally true, and what is neither. (Here come those baskets again!) But before you can ever hope to exercise your personal power to achieve your wealth, prosperity, and success, you must be able to discriminate between the three levels of truth.

Something that's accepted as true is generally in the domain of the public lexicon. Enough people believe something, and, ergo, it becomes accepted into popular language as a "truism". You've heard (and believed) many of them.

All blondes are dumb.
Kids with red hair have freckles.
Father knows best.
There's gold in them thar hills.
Every cloud has a silver lining.
If you think unhealthy thoughts,
you go to Hell.
If you're left handed, you're weird.

If you work hard, you'll be rewarded.
God helps those who help themselves.
And you can't fight City Hall.

On the other hand, a literal truth is that which is absolute, exact, precise, and faithful, and if something is "literal", then it is inarguably correct, no matter what you or anyone else may think.

As we will discuss, and consequently discover, your true power comes from within. For your world to be whole, you first have to be whole. And it is the process of doing or learning from where you get your maximum benefit, not from your achievement. These can safely be regarded as solid examples of a metaphysical - (heavenly, or spiritual) - literal truth.

But consider this.

The absolute freezing point of matter, where all molecular activity is thought to cease, is minus 273 degrees Celsius. This is a scientific literal truth called "absolute zero", and is where "all parts of the system are at the lowest energy permitted ...". The assumption is that if there is no energy, then there can be no biological growth or molecular movement. In simple terms, if you are frozen down to "absolute zero", then you will be in a state of suspended animation.

You won't get any older, you won't grow any hair or fingernails, and you'll be preserved for "ever" in the condition you were in at the time of your freezing.

The science of cryogenics was developed around this principle, and the process of freezing tissue and halting normal biogenetic life is reasonably well understood, and used in medicine routinely throughout the world.

You have probably seen the chilling images of a body packed in ice to lower its temperature, to slow the metabolic rate, while a hovering surgeon, gloved and gowned, waits anxiously for the arrival of the heart, kidney or liver that is to be transplanted. An organ that arrives in its own mini-cooler, designed to preserve the condition of the organ as close as possible to that at the time of removal from the donor body.

But one glorious day just two years ago, a group of world renowned scientists skilled in the black Art of quantum mechanics, and working in a completely different area to Medicine, got their equipment down to "absolute zero", and discovered something quite amazing. New atomic particles popped up, moved in mysterious ways like UFO's, then disappeared for all time to a place that has yet to be adequately described. (Or located, for that matter.)

Bemused, and more than a little excited, they repeated the experiment, and watched in awe as these newly discovered atomic "bits" raced around in totally unpredictable, seemingly random patterns, only to suddenly disappear leaving no proof of their existence behind!

Now all this happened in a "space" the size of a thousand Angels - about how big the head of a pin is supposed to be. And suddenly, irreversibly, from that day to this, "absolute zero" is not such an absolute, or a literal truth, any more.

The principle of chilling down living tissue to slow its degeneration is still valid, and still in common use. But the literal truth - absolute zero - what the practice of freezing human tissue was originally predicated on, is no longer as absolute as it was once thought to be.

Conversely, the literal truths of inner power, self-wholeness, and benefit-from-process were discovered by scholars and philosophers thousands of years ago, and have yet to be shown to be anything but literally true, despite the most hardened sceptic's attempts to do so over the centuries.

What is the point of all this?

Science continually pushes our knowledge of the physical world to and beyond new boundaries, constantly shattering what once in History were regarded as absolutes. In the blink of an eye, whole structures of knowledge and understanding come tumbling down, replaced with the "new" truth - challenging the next generation to push the boundaries even further.

This is the way of a dynamic world, dominated by physical reality, constantly in search of its tangible answers.

But the metaphysical truths just keep on keeping on, always constant, always available, always there for the taking and understanding.

The mystic world of the mind and the personality seem to hold more constants, more literal truths, than the physical world that encompasses them.

The point of this analogy is better understood after consideration of this simple observation.

What you take for granted forever escapes you. What you casually take to be the truth, unless it's accompanied by real understanding, is worthless, and subject to probable change.

All and any belief in the dynamic physical world is suspect, and most likely to evolve into something quite different to that which you currently assume, and expect.

And an assumed truth that you take from others or books is only of value to you if you internalise it, test it for your truth, then encompass it as part of your process, discarding its face value with all the components that do not suit your purpose.

Just as the other assumed truths mentioned earlier are of little if any consequence, so is the belief that you can't (or shouldn't) fight authority.

You can fight City Hall, because City Hall is a physical manifestation of a totally predictable structure.

City Hall is a building, constructed in such a way that only certain types of personalities can work and survive there. City Hall recognises this, and only hires those types, forever perpetuating the limitations and frustrations that make it seem such a barrier to any reasonable person.

And like anything physical, City Hall is dormant, dead, life-less, until its shadowy halls and cloistered cubicles ring to the strenuous, laboured breathing of its human occupants. People just like you, but with a different view of their professional life. A view that you must come to understand and respect, and a view that is very much pervaded by the looming unwieldy bulk of conformism.

To fight City Hall, which mostly represents all the author-ity symbols you come up against in a normal life, you must first make a genuine attempt to understand its people, and the lim-itations that City Hall places on them in their daily lives. To use your personal power to your advantage, you must first get to a position where you can use it to good effect.

And that means getting in front of the people who work for City Hall, and developing a relationship with them that allows progressive communication, or rapport. You must see the world through their eyes, from their perspective, and help them to help you.

But first you must understand where they are coming from.

When you work for City Hall, you get the power to say "NO", but you don't get the power to say "YES." The only "YES" that is allowed is one that evolves from the completion of the process, removing any form of decision making. When every box is filled in correctly, at each stage of the process, the "YES" simply means that the process may continue beyond that particular point to the next stage of the process.

All the elements of risk-taking are removed by the rigid implementation of "systems", that cannot ever be defiled or defied. The people of City Hall are highly trained in these sys-tems, and judged and promoted on how well they implement them, not on how well they solve your problem.

City Hall sees the "system" as its means of protecting itself from error, or human mistakes. If the "system" is followed exactly, then only the "right" decisions can be made, no matter how wrong or inappropriate they may turn out to be in reality.

In City Hall, common sense and reality are not mutually compatible concepts, and its people are actively discouraged from thinking about them. The system is the system, and you either fit it, and are processed, or you don't, and you are not.

The sheer size of the entrenched and vested interests that thrive in City Hall provides its unstoppable, unyielding momentum. As its people move up the narrow ladder of success, they are encouraged by their superiors to develop "empires", for the size of a department in City Hall always determines its power and influence. The more people you have working for you, the greater is your perceived contribution to the success and perpetuation of City Hall.

However, the momentum of City Hall must never be mistaken for worthwhile activity or considered performance. The sheer size of City Hall, in even its smallest manifestation, the Local Shire Council, dictates that the beast will laboriously roll along the road of life as if powered by all the devils in Hell, which may not be too far from the truth.

Any and all performance that is above the median level set by City Hall is frowned upon, and will eventually be crushed, either overtly or covertly. If a person within City Hall is ever singled out, then their future is doomed, as the potential for embarrassment at either the performance level (a subordinate does their job better than their boss), or the political level (a subordinate appears smarter or more clever than their boss), is a catastrophically negative motivational force.

Anyone, or anything, that does not fit into the general perception of who or what a City Hall subject should be, is seen as a threat, isolated, then removed. This, too, has a process, or rigid system, that guarantees a one way ticket to oblivion.

The level of threat that you may represent is measured by either the potential for confusion, the application of pressure by the use of time, or the requirement to execute in a non-procedural way. In simple terms, if you try to get City Hall to do something that is not clear to them, or you appear to be applying pressure by the use of a deadline, or what you require does not fit a system or process that allows it to proceed, then you will fail.

The classic City Hall strategy to deal with a threat is to revert to "Original Process". And the foundation of "Original Process" is decelerated time. The longer it takes, the greater the comfort level in City Hall. Conversely, the harder you push, the greater will be you difficulty in dealing with City Hall.

The degree of resistance City Hall applies to a threat is directly proportional to the height and weight of the paperwork needed to arrive at a conclusion favourable to you.

A problem that requires but the one sheet of process, generates the greatest degree of resistance, even though it may seem on the surface to present the easiest task.

Conversely, the problem that requires volumes and volumes of documentation receives very little, if any, resistance at all, because the weight of effort required to process the problem serves to justify, and therefore perpetuate, the very existence of City Hall. The more paper involved, the more automatic "YES" steps as each laborious part of the system is processed, the more comfortable City hall becomes with the outcome.

The belief is simple. The greater the process, the greater the detail, the more prolonged the agony, the less chance there is that someone will make a fatal mistake. (Fatal to City Hall, that is.)

It is City Hall's prime tenet that no criticism can ever be levelled by an outsider, if the system is followed to the letter of the Law, irrespective of the actual time it may take to do so. And because time to City Hall is simply a means of measuring the distance between pay-cheques, your time frame is of no real consequence or importance.

The longer it takes City Hall to process the system, the more likely it is that City Hall will win, even if you get the result you desire. (Because City Hall can never be seen to have made a mistake - how could they, every step of the system, every level of the process, was followed perfectly, to the absolute letter of the Law, producing the safest and only decision City Hall ever makes - the automatic one).

It is City Hall's greatest wish that the "P" word, Personality, never appear in the hallowed halls that link its humourless burrows like occluded veins in a heart patient. Personalities stand out, take sides in an argument, are likely to attempt to change things, and quite often do things that are viewed as either radical or dangerous. In a sea of calm and predictable weather, the emotional storm of an energetic, enthusiastic personality can wreck havoc on an unprecedented scale, and is to be avoided at all costs.

(Needless to say, if you are a personality, and possessed of strong measures of personal power, you must disguise yourself at first contact, letting City Hall see only what is necessary for them to understand your seriousness and good intent).

The more invisible City Hall manages to become, the better it believes it serves the community, for the biggest Sin in City Hall is not doing something wrong, or even getting caught doing something wrong. It is allowing information of the wrongdoing to get out into the Public domain, a Sin for which the perpetrator will never be forgiven.

City Hall leaks like a sieve, and uses these leaks as a means of generating and welding Power out in the Public domain. By using these leaks for your personal gain, you are empowering the hidden faces within City Hall, and executing their program for them, like a Pavlovian dog. The risk you run is that you will degrade or pollute your personal power by involving yourself with the sponge-like, intellect-dulling process that is quintessentially City Hall.

City Hall will never thank you or acknowledge you for using their leak. City Hall will always deny that a leak occurred, create a Review Committee, and prove that it did not happen, ultimately leading to the inescapable conclusion that you obtained the leaked information by illegal means!

Such Review Committees also leak like a sieve, allowing City Hall to freely publicise it's good intentions, and prove conclusively that it did not leak in the first place. Against such a circuitous process, a simple honest man has very little real resistance, irrespective of his personal power.

City Hall is at its most dangerous when it is prepared to argue its case openly, and in Public. The only time this happens is when it is impossible for the result to be in anyone's favour except City Hall. This means that the conclusion is foregone, known to all, accepted as "truth" because it is inescapable, and empowered by the general lack of will to fight it.

City Hall's greatest weapon is
reasonableness.


City Hall's greatest force is
inertia.

City Hall's biggest fear is that
someone will eventually come up with
a better system.

Consequently, City Hall is a place into which most of everything of value enters at one time or another, but precious little ever returns.

City Hall can easily be compared to a
Black Hole.

Black Hole's defy normal gravity, absorbing all energy and light within their sphere of influence. Black Holes suck in on themselves, constantly devouring everything in their path in their unending quest to absorb the Universe. So far, it would seem to be an absolute "literal" truth that nothing is bigger, or more powerful, or less understood than a Black Hole floating around somewhere out in space.

Once something falls into a Black Hole, it is never seen again. At least, that is what the scholars of our Age tell us, based on their best guesses.

There are many theories that abound about Black Holes, but very little fact. In the whole of History to this date, less than twenty published Volumes exist on the subject, and all start with the words, "..... it is postulated that ...."

What this means is that they don't
really know.

There are also many theories that abound about City Hall, and incredible volumes of facts, but for all the good it does you, it may as well be about a Black Hole. Because when it comes to dealing with City Hall, there are as many theories based on assumptions and warped opinion as there are Black Holes!

And as you already know, ".....it is postulated that......there may be hundreds - perhaps even thousands, of Black Holes......."

But you can fight City Hall, and win. One way is to have the patience of Job, time to kill, be a person of Independent Means, and start your fight early, with no expectation of a settlement within any reasonable period of time.

The other is to understand and accept City Hall for what it truly is, and remove all and any sense of frustration in trying to deal with it. By analysing City Hall's attitudes and habits, it becomes apparent that for you to win, City Hall must perceive you as no real threat to its systems; able to allow it to follow its due process; and able to cope with its awesome time demands.

You must also be able to face its people in a way that allows them to survive within City Hall, without perceived threat. This means that you must never give them a problem or information in a form that forces them to say "NO" to defend themselves or the system, or creates the need for them to have to find the person who ultimately can say "YES".

This is a degrading, humiliating exercise, for which you will get no thanks. On the contrary, you will attract the full force of City Hall's wrath, as it intuitively fights to protect its own.

Everything must be presented in a way that allows the easy application of the automatic, process driven non-decisive "YES", the one that keeps your application or problem flowing throughout the dusty corridors of assumed power. If your application or problem flows swiftly, it means that you are not a perceived or actual threat, and the speed of the process becomes an indication of the probability of a satisfactory conclusion being reached.

However, this does not always mean that you will succeed, just that your application or problem has got through the system, with a minimum of difficulty.

You need exquisite preparation, and exacting detail, and the ability to control your temperament. The realisation that you will never succeed, no matter who or what you are, or how much personal power you have developed, unless you can get City Hall to endorse your application or problem, should provide the greatest motivation for you to be in self-control.

The key issue at all times is that you never, never ask City Hall to do something that it cannot automatically do, either because of regulatory limitations, or process limitations. If you make this mistake, then the ensuing confusion will haunt your every move throughout the corridors like a deadly wraith. Always take the time to find the right section or department before you launch yourself at City Hall.

Where possible, use the City Hall reliance on systems to find out the who, what, when, where, how and why of it all, before you launch yourself into the fray. One kind word, one understanding smile to a lowly City Hall worker can bring you faster and greater rewards than an atom bomb's worth of power.

And of course, the primary consideration must always be, if at all possible, never to do anything that leads you to get involved with City Hall in the first place!

If City Hall represents Authority, in all its many forms and vested interests, then you need to seriously consider what changes in your lifestyle and your behaviour you must make to prevent City Hall from ever taking an interest in you. Generally speaking, the causal factors break out into two general types. (Here come those two baskets again!)

The first is obvious - through your efforts (or lack of effort) you break an accepted convention, and incur the wrath of The Powers That Be - City Council, Government Body, Police, Service Authority, or some equally City Hall-like bureaucracy. These types of arguments will seldom go in your favour, because City hall takes great pains to see that the minute detail involved in protecting its system is such that you either need huge, well-stuffed pockets, or a brother-in-law in the right place.

If you speed and get caught by a radar gun, even though your emotional quotient will get quite high, you must come to grips with the fact that the radar operator, and the issuing officer, are not after you personally. They are executing the policies of the day, to the best of their abilities, based on the convention that the "majority rules". No matter what your opposing attitude may be, there is simply no justification for you to have broken the convention of a speed limit.

Council ordinances are the same. Whether they be correct, fair, reasonable, well-serving, or just plain stupid is immaterial.

Because they exist, because they have been promulgated, they have the full force of City hall behind them, and woe betide the human being that flies in the face of their intent.

In essence, avoiding a clash with City Hall is the single most effective way of dealing with it. No one likes to be ignored, not even City Hall. And if it is ignored, and under-utilized, then it is quickly exposed for the self-serving fraud that it is. An empire survives and thrives on process and system, but if you remove the need for either, then the whole top-heavy structure will come tumbling down.

The second type of causal factor is more insidious. When City Hall comes-a-calling, watch out! Why would City Hall come to you? A prolific number of reasons, from inspecting a Public Facility, like gas, water, electricity, fences, boundaries, to compliance with regulations, and field work to assess the potential for threat from the unknown. Irrespective of the reason, if you trip up the person from City Hall, become entangled in a debate with them, or take a stance that clearly suggests that they should cease and desist, then you will create a psychological phenomenon called "Fight or Flight".

If City Hall runs, or is seen to retreat, you can expect the full majesty of its repugnant, immovable, unyielding bureaucratic might to descend on your head, and not necessarily just in the area you offended. Worse, if City Hall decides to fight you there and then, outside the corridors of power, then you are in real trouble. Sit back, relax, and let the process begin, and try to keep your sense of humour at all costs, because the more emotion you show, the greater their perceived victory!

Like a bellowing tractor with a locked-up gear box, the only thing that will stop or slow City Hall is when it runs out of steam - vents its collective anger, and regroups to assess what it has to do to appear conciliatory.

And, as we saw before, City Hall is never more dangerous than when it appears to be reasonable.

When the lull does come, then it's time for some well tested tactics.

You fight fire with fire, detail with detail, summons with response. You must show them that you can master their process, meet their demands, and comply with their regulations. You must demonstrate that you can match them page for page, line for line, meeting for meeting. You must always remove the perceived threat, or even the possibility of a threat. Unless you do this, why then, "You can't fight City Hall!"

The moral to all this can be found in an intriguing story taken from the Mayan Scrolls, unearthed just ten years ago deep in the Konya Valley. How ancient scrolls from a South American culture managed to find their way into the foot of Turkey, is not yet clear. But what is clear, is that even back then, two and a half thousand years ago, City Hall loomed large in the life of the ordinary man!

"In the year 455 BC," or so the story goes, " a simple herder, herding a flock of motley goats along a well-worn path suddenly came upon a rock, which was so massive it blocked his easy passage. Sitting next to the rock was a Tax Collector, brewing java over an open flame. He looked up as the approach of the smelly herder blocked his sun, and smiled, gesturing at a small patch of flat mud to his side.

"Would you care to sip with me, old man?" he asked politely. The herder sighed, looked around to confirm that his goats had not wandered, and bowed gratefully, using his gnarled staff to lower his ancient bones to the ground.

The Tax Collector poured the rank black liquid into a small earthen cup, and offered it to his guest.

"This is a fine aroma," the herder commented, sniffing the wafting steam that rose from the small cup. He bowed his thanks, and sipped. The Tax Collector mimicked his guest, drawing in the vapour through well-used nostrils, then sipped gently at the rim of his cup. The sun, tired after its day-long journey across the cloud flecked sky, sunk gratefully behind the mottled hills, casting long shadows across the track.

"You know," the herder commented, in a wishful voice, "it is not fair and proper that the District Legionnaire collect a tithe from a poor working man, simply so that he may go around an obstruction, carefully placed by the Gods to test his mettle, and be on his way. It is simply not fair."

The Tax Collector looked into the rheumy eyes of the old man, and smiled again, offering more java as he did so.

"You are not being taxed to pass the rock, old man," he said gently, pouring the sweet black liquid into the herder's cup, "an Act of the Gods is an Act of the Gods, and let no man place a value upon it." The herder bent to his cup, thinking, then raised his head, one eyebrow cocking quizzingly.

"Then why a Tax Collector, even such a nice one as yourself, at this exact spot?" he asked. The Tax Collector laughed, carefully placing the boiling pot back on the fire, stoking it with a broken shoot of burnt bamboo.

"Old man, it should be obvious. If indeed the Gods went to all this trouble to create an impasse, why, then, we must honour Them with recognition, and celebrate Their mighty feat." The herder shook his head, not understanding this explanation in the slightest. He slowly stood, his rickety frame unfolding itself like a rusted erector set.

"Then if you are not here to tax me, I will humbly thank you for your hospitality, and be on my way." The Tax Collector smiled, and rose to look the herder in the eye. He placed one arm on his shoulder, in the style of greeting that was in vogue at the time, and placed his other hand palm up below his chin, fingers pointing at the other man's heart.

"With my blessings, old man, with my blessings. Just as soon as you have paid for your tea!"

Like Death itself, some say, you cannot escape the Tax man. And the Tax man works for City Hall.

So what really is City hall? It's no more than an attitude, one formed from the process of conformity. We are all expected to conform to accepted norms within the society in which we live, and just like the difficulties you sometimes experienced growing up with your parents, as you mature and develop your personal power you are sure to have the occasional brush with City Hall.

It's like falling rain. It's great when it comes at the end of a long hot spell, but it's a nuisance on top of a deluge that has flooded your yard. Affirmation by City Hall that you are a good and worthwhile citizen is a life-enriching experience. A traffic ticket, parking notice, speeding fine, or code violation is simply the system reminding you that for the good of the majority, rules have been agreed to, and you have transgressed these rules, to your detriment.

Now, understanding where real personal power comes from, and being a student of experiential learning, how hard a problem is that to overcome?

So you can fight City Hall, after all.

Can't you?

# THE CUNNING OF THE FOX

One of the secrets of personal power
is in knowing who you really are.
In this respect, the humble Fox
is an interesting study.

The unlucky Fox, in the good days past, got to snug up against the skin of all the most beautiful women in the world. He or she was skinned and stretched into a pelt, then hand stitched into a warm coat, and worn not necessarily for comfort, but for show. They also got to be chased by the most expensive horses in the land, barked at by the most pedigreed dogs, and shot at by the soberest and most proper of gentlemen.

Now this, mind you, was the unlucky Fox!

The lucky Fox missed out on all this sport and luxury, preferring to use his cunning and guile to eat well, and live long.

The principles of survival emulated by the Fox bear close examination, for how often do you see some poor person's ego mounted on someone else's horse, being displayed for all to see?

In fact, how often have you felt that your precious ego has been temporarily possessed or controlled by another person, and you've all but been powerless to stop it?

Let's look at the Fox, and see what lessons you can apply to your own life, and the development of your personal power.

For starters, the Fox has a very clear perspective of who and what he (she) is. He (she - he will do from now on, the point on sexual equality is either made by now, or never can be!) is a smallish four legged animal, with a big bushy tail, pointed nose, deep black eyes with sharp focus, excellent developed sense of smell, good reflexes, good burst of speed, and medium endurance.

Now never expect a Fox to tell you all this - they are what they are, well, because they are. And lacking any need to be something else, they always are what they appear to be.

A Fox uses all his skills and instincts, to the fullest of his ability. He doesn't shirk from a fight, but avoids them if he can. He has a highly developed sense of society, but is equally capable of surviving on his own. He only kills what he needs to eat, and is perfectly happy to share his conquests with other Foxes. He guards his young, sees to their development and survival, and accepts their growth and independence as a fact of life.

They may never know that the title we have given them is "Fox". However, their instincts are such, that from the day they are born, until the day they die, they act, think, hunt, eat, move, sleep, mate, and live, as a Fox is supposed to.

Why? Because that is how we see them acting, and it appears that they don't know any different way to act. (Notice that it is the point of view of the observer that determines what we see and think, not what the observed thinks or feels). The Fox doesn't stop to examine his role in life, he just gets on and lives it. He doesn't make anything special about what he does instinctively, he just does the same things over and over again, in the fiercely competitive world he lives in.

In Nature, like everything else, there is a natural order, and what the observer sees is the interaction of the various species within a given environment. The human need to quantify and qualify, to unravel the secrets of the Universe, created the need to define and title, to understand and label, hence all things that look and act like a Fox are called "Fox".

But what makes this work for us is an external observation, based on experiential learning. The poor Fox, lacking the ability to read, choose, and develop personal power, has no option but to be a Fox. To be observed by us being a Fox, and consequently judged by us on how good a Fox he really is.

To the Fox, survival is his only reward. Starting and growing a whole lot of little Foxes is but a passing need, dictated by instinct, to protect the species labelled "Fox" from extinction. (Not that he knows this of course, he is only answering the call of nature). Concepts like heat, cold, wet or dry are but passing phases for one who lives in the hollowed tree stump, or carefully sculptured lair.

When one temporary home becomes untenable, for whatever reason, he simply moves on, and establishes another. Personal possessions are unnecessary, but staking out his "turf" is of prime importance.

He demands and gets respect from other Foxes, until he is perceived as weak. Then he will either be killed, or left to die on his own. And just like us, Foxes don't take anything with them when they die. Not that they would if they could.

In getting comfortable with this information, and so long as the Fox acts like our perception of a Fox, we become essentially happy, and our curiosity, for the time at least, is abated. We know all there is to know about the Fox, and nothing stands out as a puzzle or a threat.

But should the Fox suddenly start acting like a Chicken, then all Hell will break loose!

"It can't do that!" we rage, reaching for the nearest shotgun.

"How dare it pretend to be a Chicken!" we shout, unleashing the Dogs of War.

Our fury knows no bounds, and our emotional levels rise to new heights. Simply because our perception of reality has been challenged, and by a dumb animal, no less!

The first secret of the Fox is a simple one.

You, as the observer, determine what your reality will be. It is as you see it, experience it, taste it, visualize it, and finally, internalise it.

If you want to be rich, and you believe that you will be rich, and act like you want to be rich, then you will become rich.

Now, you balked at a Fox trying to be a Chicken. A Fox is not gifted with wisdom, the ability to choose, the ability to develop personal power. A Fox is a Fox is a Fox.

But you can be anything you choose to be, whenever you choose to be it.

Want to be a politician? Easy. Want real wealth? Easy. Want fabulous success? Easy. Want to take control of your life, and prosper? Easy.

Learn from the Fox.

"Animal cunning" is a metaphor you have heard often, and most times the person who uses this phrase does so with a wishful sound in their voice, as if they wanted this magical Animal cunning for themselves, to use in some part of their lives.

Animal cunning is no more than basic instinct, one usually honed around a strong desire to survive. This is a primitive, but enormously powerful, motivating force, and if you examine it closely, it is no more than a statement about "self". You must be preserved. You must be perpetuated. You must be honoured. You must be recognised. You must be a pivotal force in your Universe.

So what is stopping you?

The Fox travels through life instinctively, reacting to the forces of Nature. He is a moving, predetermined entity in a random environment, and how well he survives depends on how well and how quickly he adapts. He cannot control his environment, and is at the mercy of the natural order of things. (Every species has a natural enemy, designed by God to prevent one species dominating the world. A question of balance.)

You, however, have the ability to decide what you want for yourself, and manipulate your environment accordingly. You can choose to be anything you want to be, and become it, simply by initiating positive actions that take you toward your goal. You must have the desire to become what you want to be. A desire so strong you can taste it.

And because you can taste it, you can become utterly convinced that it is possible, no matter what anyone else may think or say. And the moment you convince yourself that your goal is true, it becomes your reality, and all you need do to make it happen is to make it happen.

The biggest single factor in determining your personal power is your belief in what you do. And belief comes from the strength of your vision and commitment.

You can create reality - you are the observer - you are the one who determines what is what. If it is not real to you, then it is not real. But if it is real to you, then you can empower your vision with the strength of your belief and commitment and see your reality come true.

This is a mind power thing, and many good books have been written about it. But the essence of the understanding is that you recall the image of the Fox - in your mind, he can never be a Chicken, because you have predetermined what the characteristics of a Fox are.

Change those determinations, change your perceptions, and you can change you beliefs. If you change your beliefs, then you can change reality.

And a Fox can become a Chicken.

And you can become anything in the world you want to be, any time you choose to.

Another attribute of the Fox is that he has a clearly defined comfort zone, out of which he rarely moves, if at all.

Again, he is instinctively protecting himself from a harsh environment he has no control over, and very little understanding of, beyond his needs to survive.

This comfort zone is like a barrier to the outside world, both protecting the Fox from unexpected surprises, and protecting the outside world from the Fox becoming a Chicken. If he ever does make the switch, then he moves us out of our comfort zone, threatening our perceptions and beliefs, as we have discovered earlier.

However, we can actively change the self-imposed limits of our comfort zone, considerably enhancing our ability to achieve the things in life we hold so dear - wealth, prosperity, success and personal power.

First, you have to determine what and where the existing boundaries of your comfort zone are. This is easy, just ask yourself the following questions - What am I most afraid of? Success? Failure? Ignorance? Disability? Lack of stature? Poverty? Sickness? Relationships? Something else?

Your honest answers will provide a guide to where your current comfort zone is. Fear is an emotion, and easily soothed by understanding. True understanding removes barriers for you, whenever the understanding is applied in an honest way. Just like being scared of the dark is temporarily fixed by turning on a light.

Your fear of the dark hasn't gone, just the dark.

You can also expand your comfort zone by a quick influx of knowledge. However, to gain any permanency in this expansion, you have to internalise your new understanding, and make it a part of your truth.

If you are afraid of success, as many people are (but don't know it), then you will have an inbuilt resistance to achieving your goals. You've seen people like this, they always seem to shoot themselves in the foot just as they are about to achieve great things. "What a pity" we all say in sympathy, not realising that some hidden inner subconscious force determined their downfall.

Now the Fox doesn't have this problem. Not being the possessor of great intellect, he operates on instinct, and uses his senses to keep him out of trouble. But we humans constantly strive for things that are just out of our reach, many times without knowing the ramifications of what we are doing, blindly ignoring our instincts.

This is the second great secret of the Fox

Tread carefully, and slowly, until you understand the dynamics of what it is you are striving to do. Sniff the winds of change, search out the mysteries of your environment, and use all your senses to determine your course of action. Consider all the options, and, if necessary, and practical, try the lot. The only limitation you have is the one you place on yourself.

For once you have decided on what you really want, and visualised it so strongly that it has become your truth, you must take the time to learn how best you can achieve you new ambition. Not instinctively, like the Fox, but purposefully, like a visionary with a magic dream. And in a manner and a fashion that is true to your instincts, because you cannot change who you are, only what you may become.

We are each born with a bucket of ability, always available for us to dip into. The raw talents and intuitions can be honed and expanded, but the basic "I" can never be altered. You are who you are, and can never be someone else. But you can change what you do with your life, and what you become in it.

Like the Fox, you will never get away with trying to be a Chicken.

But you can successfully emulate what the Chicken does, and benefit from the experience.

Foxes are often trapped by things that look and smell correct, but are fatally flawed. These "baits" come in many forms, the most common being the classic piece of poisoned meat, rich and succulent, enough to make the strongest jowls dribble with anticipation. Because the Fox is instinctive, he is all too readily taken by the external trappings of an easy, attractive meal. It is not until he has consumed his fill that the acid suddenly turns to bile, and his guts vomit the poison back up, in a last ditch attempt to save him.

Human history is riddled with metaphors that accurately describe this phenomenon - all the way back to the Trojan

Horse. "There's no such thing as a free lunch" is a modern day equivalent. Thus the third secret is revealed. You get nothing for nothing. Beware of the easy solution, the quick fix, the promise of riches, the almost Irresistible lure of instant fame and fortune.

The path to glory is booby-trapped with hundreds of "baits", all poised to take the unwary, unthinking pilgrim, who confuses opportunity with ambition. Because it is your truth that you are attempting to give life to - it is your vision of what you want to achieve for yourself - it is extremely unlikely that a ready-made, instant, easy, immediate solution exists, that you can just step up and take without cost.

You get in this life what you pay for. The people you most respect are those that have achieved great things - they weren't given them, they went out and got them with energy, vision, and great effort.

You must do the same.

If the Fox wants to eat, he must hunt. If he wants to sleep soundly, he must build a lair. If he wants to survive, he must avoid his enemies. It's only when he gets lazy, and takes an easy bait, that he gets himself into real trouble.

Trouble that can easily be fatal for a simple Fox.

As the Fox stretches out in the Sun, letting the warmth revitalise his tired muscles, his tongue lolls out one side of his mouth, and he pants, his black eyes roving the horizon. Every so often, he stops this, points his long snout at the sky, and sniffs the air. Even at rest, he is crucially aware of his environment, and those in it who would threaten him and his pack. He has many natural enemies, and just as many unnatural ones.

And like other dog-like animals, he uses his unique smell to wet down trees and shrubs, letting other Foxes know that this particular piece of turf is his, and that they should stay away.

Unfortunately, this specific odour is also his greatest weakness, because many of the predatory animals who rate Fox as their number #1 choice for dinner have a highly developed sense of smell, and easily locate their unfortunate prey by finding where he urinated, and track him to his lair.

This is the Fox's biggest secret. He doesn't understand (because no one has told him) how his enemies find him, but he soon realises that unless he is ever vigilant, he will soon be the centre-piece in someone's banquet. He is constantly on the alert, never taking anything for granted, always wary of a new scent or odour, suspicious about anything that is out of place, and curious about anything that doesn't look and smell right.

So must you on your chosen path to wealth, prosperity, fame and personal power.

Always have an enquiring mind, always seek the truth in what you observe, never take anything for granted, and always be on the look-out for new understanding. In this way, the natural wisdom of the Fox can be yours, and where all he gets is survival as his reward, you will get the power of your vision, and the ability to make your dreams come true!

In the days of conquest ahead, always remember the cunning of the Fox, and his secrets, and what they can do for you.

Never take anything for granted. Always make new knowledge and experience a part of your truth, empowering your intellect to the fullest.

Be on the look-out for false symbols, and empty promises. And never, never, take a poisoned bait.

Tread carefully, in small measures, at least until you fully understand the full ramifications of your actions.

And be what you are meant to be, not what others project you to be. Learn from their expectations, but profit from your considered opinion.

Realise that the world is full of promise and opportunity, just as it is full of black pits and snares.

Think of the Fox often, and learn from his highly tuned instincts.

And consider the possible consequences if you do not!

# LOST IN SPACE

Your intellect can wander
through the heavens,
occasionally peeking at a Star,
or it can rocket through the Universe,
latched onto the tail of a Comet.
The big step is overcoming
the limitations
of the speed of light!

What really is "intellect"? Is it how smart you are, or appear to be? Is it a measurement of your cleverness? Has it something to do with how witty you may be?

Yes, and no.

A close scrutiny of the word shows us that "intellect" is defined as comprehension, or ability to understand; ability to reason, or to discriminate; insight; intuition; perception; sensitivity. It is clearly a grab-bag of many emotions, feelings, and character traits.

Your eyes are regarded as the window to your soul. They are also, along with your ears and your other senses, the doors to your intellect. Unfortunately, the outlets for your intellect are your mouth, and your body, or what you demonstrate physically in the way you do and say things.

The word "intellect" is usually associated with clever people, geniuses, or those much smarter than we are. In truth, we all have the same God given ability to develop our intellect, if only we choose to do so.

And developing your intellect is a fundamental requirement of developing your maximum personal power. The two go hand in hand, and you can't have one without the other.

It is true that some people seem to have a greater mental capacity, or are able to learn things easier, than others. It is also true that some people seem to develop their intellect better than others. But the fact remains that anyone can choose to develop their intellect, to whatever level you desire.

Comprehension is simply your ability to understand things that you read, hear, or observe. How well you comprehend is determined by many factors, such as your present frame of reference, the accuracy of the input, the state of your mental faculties, your desire to process the information, and your ability to filter what you learn into its component parts.

Your frame of reference is dependent on your experience, and your retained memory of things. If you've never read or heard about a small animal called a Fox before, then the first time you see one, you won't know what it is. You will have no comprehension of what you should call it, or do with it. If you have heard of it before, but have forgotten what you learned, then you will still be confused, and uncertain. Two words that you know rob you of your personal power.

It is possible to have a very wide, general-purpose frame of reference, simply by reading extensively, and staying in tune with your environment. Newspapers, magazines, books, Current Affairs programmes, and computer-accessed data bases all offer a wealth of information, on literally any subject you choose to pursue. The greater your frame of reference, the greater will be your comprehension, and the greater will be the development of your personal power.

It has often been said, that there is nothing more powerful than an informed person, able to share their knowledge with those around them. You will never hear this statement refuted by anyone who is really successful, but you may well hear it challenged by those who are not.

The accuracy of what you absorb, is dependent on two factors. The first, and most obvious, is the absolute truth of the information you are receiving. If you are reading, then the written word needs to be factual, or understood as stimulative. If you are watching TV, then the pictures need to be unbiased, and honest in their construction. If you are listening, then what you hear needs to be unfettered with colour and personality. And if you are feeling, then the sensory perception must match what the other object is really transmitting.

The second factor is a little more complex, and it's all to do with you. When you are exposed to data, you tend to automatically filter what you see, hear, and feel, by what you expect, have experienced previously, or believe to be true. There's nothing wrong with this process, in fact, it's vital that you do apply these filters to everything, or you'd be swamped to the point of numbness by untold volumes of irrelevant data.

The issue is how true you are being in applying these filters. If you are limited by what you know, you deny yourself access to new knowledge. If you are prejudiced towards what is being communicated, then you will colour it with your negative attitude. And if you are applying the limit of what you have experienced previously, then you will prevent the synergistic process of stimulation from occurring, reducing the potential of the new experience adding to your reservoir of understanding.

All this is controlled by the state of your mental faculties, or how perceptive and receptive you are willing to be. Just as people only learn what they want to learn, and when they want to learn it, you will only be receptive to new knowledge when you want to be. Your receptiveness is directly related to your energy levels, your thirst for knowledge, and your desire to succeed.

By looking at you, others can easily judge the state of your intellect. If you carry an easy smile, your eyes sparkle with truth and trust, and your body is alive with energy, then it is obvious that your intellect is comfortably maxing it to the limit. Just this persona grants you a serious measure of personal power, before you even say or do anything, to either confirm the truth of the observation, or destroy it.

Confidence breeds its own success.

To be receptive, you must be at peace with yourself and your environment. Your energy must be centred in your Paradise, and you must be capable of accepting the new knowledge for what it is, not what you want it to be. Your attitude needs to be that of the observer, not the judge. You need to have the biggest ears in the world, and the willingness to use them. And you must be able to discern what it is you are really hearing, seeing, or feeling, not necessarily just what it appears to be.

The ability to process is vital to your growth as a whole person. Take a leaf out of the Ancient Scholar's Book, and start with the two baskets. One for what is, and one for what might be. Actively apply your experience to the data, sifting through it for things that taste right. Examine them minutely, then swallow them into your consciousness.

That which you cannot use, don't like the taste of, or don't understand yet, tip into the second basket, to await their turn. Some will arise at a later date because of new information that allows them to become useful. Others will call you like a siren, demanding that you take the time and effort to understand them, and learn from them. The rest is better off left where it is, because your lifetime is finite, and not only do you not need to know everything in the world, you couldn't if you tried!

Once you have accepted information, filter it into its component parts, storing all the bits in the different parts of your memory and experiential data banks, for future use. But above all else, grow to enjoy the process, because learning is a dynamic activity, one that has the ability to charge your ego with short-term stimulation, and flush your soul with the power of new truth. People who are truly alive learn something new every minute of every day, every day of their achievement-filled lives.

That's why they are successful.

Knowledge is power. The more you know, the more power you will have. And it's not just the ability to know things that is important. Knowledge protects you from attack, because if your have developed your intellect, you are less likely to be tricked, fooled, be taken in by a lie, or led down the dark path of deceit and evil.

Your ability to reason or discriminate is something that grows with your experience. In many ways, how well you reason something out, or apply your discriminatory process, controls the amount of time you need to absorb new learning. The faster you can reason, the more you can learn. The better you discriminate, the least amount of time you waste chasing ghosts.

There is a dark side to reason, and it can often lead to misunderstanding and frustration. When someone tells you that what you are saying sounds "reasonable", what they are really saying is that they either aren't sure of what it is you have said, and they are considering it further, or that it hasn't threatened them at any conscious or unconscious level. Unfortunately, we often hear this as acceptance of what we are striving to achieve, rather than as a request for more information.

You know that a "reasonable" person is not always the one you would trust with your life, or your future. Don't know why, but the very reasonableness of "reasonable" seems to depower it, the moment the word is used to describe a person, rather than a process!

Insight, or the knowledge that comes from within you, as part of your truth, is what fuels your ability to be clever and shrewd. An insightful person is one who is regarded as being on the ball, quick to take advantage of opportunities, and one who generates a lot of respect for their ability to rapidly understand and communicate well. This is the first of the attributes that is also influenced by your skill levels. The greater your personal skills, the more insight you can bring to bear on a problem.

And the more insight you have available, the greater and more efficient is your ability to process. Understanding, learning, experience, wisdom and unfulfilled curiosity funnel stimulus towards your inner self, and as you become more efficient and more discriminatory in how you handle the influx of information, you empower your insight to work for you, autonomously.

Intuition is something quite different. When you think you know something, but you're not sure why or how you know, you are exercising your intuitive ability. This is a "feeling" thing rather than a physical thing, and is very much up to the individual as to how much you have, and how often you can use it.

It takes great trust and belief in yourself to let your intuition guide you, because many times there is nothing to show but a vague "feeling" of uneasiness, or a warm glow of positive reassurance. Intuition is totally in the mind, and its usefulness is dependent on the state of your mental health, your inner stance, your energy levels, and your truth.

When you are powerful, your intuition will serve you well. When you are not, it will simply not be there, because intuition is generated by the positive side of your nature, and driven by your subconscious mind. You cannot dictate to it, you cannot call it up on demand, and you cannot force it to obey your will.

It is either there, or it is not, and the harder you try, the further away it will get. Conversely, the more you learn, the longer you study, the better your understanding becomes, the greater will be your intuitive abilities. The more at peace you become with yourself, the harder you chase down your goals, and the more energetic you get at developing your personal power, the better your intuition will serve you.

Perception is a many edged sword within your personality. It involves your awareness, your consciousness, your powers of observation, the depth and breadth of your vision, and your keenness to get amongst the swimming pools of life. As you grow stronger and more aware, your perception heightens.

How aware you are goes all the way back to your desire and focus. If you want to achieve something hard enough, then you will generate the desire within you to motivate you to get the job done, and done well. As your desire increases in intensity, your awareness of all around you increases, erg for erg. In a sense, the more aware you become, the more perceptive you are, because awareness is the secondary building block (after desire) to achievement.

The observer in you, the voyager, the adventurer, the seeker of knowledge, will always strive to heighten your awareness. And as your awareness reaches its peak, so does your ability to absorb new understanding. The keener your awareness, the greater the quality of what you take in to be your truth.

Your state of consciousness, or your span of attention, is all to do with how well, and how long, you can concentrate on something. There are many different elements at work here, all the way from your physical fitness level, your inner stance, the level of your desire, the degree of your commitment, the perceived difficulty of the task, how well you have created your strategy, the simplicity of your tactics, and the amount of willpower you can allocate to achieving your goal.

You will learn what you want to learn, at a time when you most want to learn it. It is that simple. And your attention span, or consciousness, will exactly match your commitment to the task.

Your powers of observation wax and wane with your arousal levels. To observe is not just to "see", it is also to think, internalise, compare, filter, judge, absorb, relate, accept and use wisely the information you are gathering from your senses. How well you can do this at any one time is dependent on all the other things you are trying to do.

There is a classic military situation that exactly fits this state of mind. It is called "Situational Awareness", and it is the result of two factors - training and stress.

Way back at the start of the century, aeroplanes were stately things flown by adventurous people. They were essentially simple devices, made from wood and fabric, and were so stable that some almost "flew" themselves. Just as many ended up as piles of burning rubble, as the more adventurous pilots attempted to push back the barriers of aeronautical knowledge, giving up their lives in the process.

The DH82 Tiger Moth, famous as a World War 2 trainer, is one such aircraft, and it flies sedately along at 85 knots. Once the pilot has mastered its peculiar quirks, he only has to watch three instruments to know where he is, and stay right-side up, for as long as his fuel, or the call of the clear blue sky lasts.

The Tiger Moth holds its place in history not just for the valuable role it played in the Allied War effort, but in the fact that as aeroplanes go, it is a classic. Simple to fly, true to its pilots, and able to survive 60 years and longer on the strength of its unique character.

But the simplicity of the Tiger Moth evolved into the complexity of the legendary Spitfire and Hurricane, Mustang and Hell Cat, and the three primary instruments were replaced with switches, dials, radios, pumps, levers, and a multitude of complex procedures. Finally, jet-propelled coffins with tiny wings, ripped up the sky faster than the naked eye could follow.

Today, the lucky pilot    of a jet fighter under combat conditions is faced with the awesome task of monitoring up to three hundred different instruments, switches and radios, fly his aircraft, watch his radar, monitor his threat receivers, find the enemy, keep track of his own people, and avoid flying into the ground while not getting lost, or getting disorientated at night or in bad weather. And all this must be done while zooming around the sky at up to 1,450 nautical miles per hour!

During the evolution of the modern jet fighter, the military very quickly established the need to create an extensive training regime, where all the uncertainty could be removed from the demanding task of maximising the pilot's performance. They found that the sheer weight of what the average pilot was expected to do exceeded most people's ability, without massive training.

By attending to every little detail, analysing the human-factors requirements, and the ergonomics of the jet cockpit, they devised a series of procedures to handle each single activity. In effect, they broke down every action into its component parts, and prioritised every step.

They then trained the pilots until they could fly and fight by instinct, and recite the procedures off by heart. The pilots were bundled into ground-based simulators, where they practiced every manoeuvre under the pressure they could expect when flying in real conditions. This process removed ninety-five percent of the workload modern technology had forced on them, and allowed the pilot to focus on what is the most important thing in his life - staying in front of his speeding jet, and his enemy, and consequently, staying alive.

The pilot doesn't have to watch three hundred instruments, he only has to scan them fleetingly, noticing only those that are outside normal limits. Because every aspect of flying the speeding aircraft is ingrained in his memory (both mind and muscle), he is freed up to keep his head outside the cockpit, scanning the skies for the bad guys.

The application of mental pressure, induced by the necessity of getting home alive, heightens his awareness and his powers of observation, which would be severely limited if he still had to mechanically watch everything, think about every little detail, and fly the aircraft at the same time.

Ask any jet pilot when he "sees" the best, when his awareness is at its highest, when his vision is the purest, and when his mind is full of clarity, and invariably he will give you one of two answers.

When he is threatened with a bogey on his tail, or when he is in a terminal area, amongst other aircraft, and about to land back on either his carrier or runway.

These are the two times of maximum arousal, and maximum stress, when his survival is on the line, and a mistake could cost him more than just a slap on the wrist.

If he gets caught by a bad guy, he gets shot down. In a terminal area, fast jets congregate in large numbers, both landing and taking off, and the possibility of an aerial collision increases dramatically.

Any lapse in concentration, and any time his head is looking inside the cockpit at his dials and instruments, robs him of his ability to "see" outside. It could well cost him his life.

But what allows him to use his situational awareness to the fullest, is the incredible extent of his training. Everything is ingrained in his subconscious, to the point where he can do it literally in his sleep. All the pressure of the moment does, is focus his attention where he needs it the most - outside the cockpit, intently scanning the few million cubic metres of sky he is responsible for.

His "situational awareness" allows him to fly his complex aircraft without necessarily thinking about it, while he retains his ability to maximise his outward looking focus. In effect, this is a "super-human" performance, because without his training, the task would be almost impossible to achieve.

Likewise, if you break down your strategy into simple tactics, then analyse which actions can be "trained" into your system, then you too, just like the fighter pilot, can enjoy a high level of situational awareness.

The more aroused you become about what it is that you are doing, the better your powers of observation will be. The more you "see", the more you take in and understand, the greater the knowledge you gain.

And it is axiomatic that as you get better and better at the process of discovery, the greater will be your advantage, and the better prepared you will be to face uncertainty and confusion.

Sensitivity is a well-worn word, and one that, until just a few years ago, was very much out of fashion in the macho, male ego-dominated world. Yet true sensitivity is the one reliable precursor to great intellect.

Just as you can never hope to attain your fullest personal power without doing the real work, or achieve the maximum benefits of it without force-multiplying, you can never achieve your intellectual potential without developing great sensitivity. This emotional awareness is what will put you in tune with your Universe, help you to find your harmony within your environment, and create the basis for your inner peace, and consequently, your inner stance.

You can learn to be more sensitive, more considerate, more tolerant, more giving, but first you have to honestly assess, like watching the dial of a radio, where exactly your sensitivity is on a scale of 1 to 100.

Research over the past twenty years shows that the average "degree" of male sensitivity, when measured against 40 standard parameters, is slowly increasing from a mean "36" to a present mean of "46". To be successful in your relationship with other people, you need to be at least in the high 60's!

The one person you most admire in your life is the most sensitive person you know. Where would you place them on the scale? Now, where would you place yourself, compared to them?

Sensitivity has a lot to do with the little things in life. In fact, the smaller and more insignificant the task or thing appears, the greater the sensitivity required to acknowledge it, and honour it with your intellect. Most times, you relate your sensitivity to how you feel about someone, or how they have dealt with you.

This emotional barometer has very little to do with real sensitivity, it is just an emotional spark in an otherwise dull day.

True sensitivity is a mindset, an all-encompassing attitude, a vital part of your bearing and your external stance, and persona. You can't switch it on and off like a light bulb, you either have it, or you don't. But just like wisdom allows you to properly exercise your personal power, sensitivity allows you to truly develop your intellect to its fullest potential.

Again, you can't have one without the other.

Sound travels around the world at approximately 720 miles per hour. (approximately 1,200 kilometres per hour). Light flashes around the Universe at approximately 186,000 miles every second. (That's an astonishing 298,000 kilometres every second!)

When you talk, you speak at the speed
of sound.

When you think, you work at the speed
of light.

Consequently, energy used to think is 928,800 times better used, than the same amount of energy used to talk. Your mouth actually reduces your capacity to achieve things!

The synapse's in your brain, the little electronic connections that link all the cells together - the dark places where all your memory, intellect, and motion controllers live - spark constantly at the speed of light - 186,000 miles every second. This means that you have an enormous intellectual capacity, one that has to be seen to be believed.

Research shows that most people, in their entire lifetime, only ever use 13% of their brain capacity. Yet the key to your very being is rooted in your cerebral cortex, which is the basis of the brain's intellectual capacity, the seat of learning and memory, and a centre for associative functions, for many sensory perceptions, and for many motor activities.

Simply put, it's where the "real" you lives! And like any energy-dependent activity, if you don't use it, you lose it.

Your opportunity is limitless.

Develop your intellect, and you
develop your mind.
Develop your mind, and you develop
your personal power.
Develop your personal power, and you can achieve all the wealth, prosperity, and success you could ever want!

And now that you know what intellect is, what's stopping you?

As one wise scholar once said, long before the knife of the surgeon first revealed the quivering grey mass that is central to our powers, "The heart is where the desire is, but the head is where the action is!"

So use your head.

# ONE PLUS ONE EQUALS TEN

The concept of force-multiplication
is as old as the hills,

but it still seems to confuse
a lot of very good people.
Without it,
you can never develop
your personal power
to the max.

Imagine for one second that you are a Roman soldier in the time of Pompei, standing in the desert heat, massive shield on one arm, pointed lance proudly astride the other. Through the thin slits of your face-protecting helmet, a flurry of dust rising majestically on the far horizon briefly catches your eye.

Then, on the swirl of a welcome breeze, the faint pounding of horses' hooves reaches you, and you start to wonder.

You're wearing the very latest in soldiering gear - brass striped skirt-like armour, a brass chest plate, helmet, and leather boots with brass strappings. If you have to run, you'll be weighed down by the very things that are supposed to protect you.

Intuitively, you know you're no match for a soldier on horseback, but orders are orders, and you grit your teeth, gird your loins, and lean into your spear, ready to take the charge.

When the dust settles, the last shriek from a dying horse carrying the battlefield, smoke and the stink of death fill your nostrils, and shaking the hot, dry sand from your battle dress, you swear by all that's Holy that the very next day you'll take riding lessons, and hang the expense!

The reality is that which was supposed to most protect you, your brass armour, weighed you down, reduced your ability to move and run, limited your options, and dictated how you fought a superior, more mobile, enemy.

This is the exact same experience you will have every time you allow yourself to be limited by what you think you know.

Knowledge and experience are the two major building blocks in the development of your personal power, but they can also be the cause of your downfall. The moment you assume something, you limit your potential, reduce your vision, filter your hearing, and dull your senses. You effectively pre-program your intellect to expect certain things, and automatically reject anything that doesn't fit your preconceptions.

The three most useless things in life are the knowledge you leave behind you, the experience you casually pass by, and the wisdom you never develop.

You must have the outlook and awareness of an observer, sensitive to all around you. You must be the seeker of knowledge, and you must constantly empower your intellect with new stimulus.

Thus went the foot soldier in favour of the horseman.

The realisation that the body armour was indeed necessary to prevent the arrow or the lance from easily penetrating your skin, drove you onto the back of a horse, so that you could regain your mobility. No sooner had you done this than a new challenge appeared on the horizon, one that effortlessly seemed to be able to cope with your new found power.

Enter the charioteer.

Not one man, but two. And anything up to six horses, frothing at the mouth, powering their stylish cart around at frightening speeds. And, seemingly, almost magically, these two charioteers had the killing ability of ten men.

They moved faster than anyone else on the battlefield, they protected each other from blind-side attacks, they used their horses and carts as shields, battering rams, and (horse-powered) steam rollers. And the blades they attached to their wheels carved the legs out from under the hapless foot soldiers thrown casually into their path.

Still only two men, but with enhancement of their personal power, able to fight like ten.

The advent of technology saw spears and swords give way to bows and arrows, which in time were replaced (thanks to the Chinese) by bombs and bullets. An arrow is simply a flying spear, that is propelled further than a man can physically throw - a kind of force-multiplication effect that allows his "range", or killing area - to expand.

The bullet is just a faster, better, smaller arrow, that again extended the distance between the soldier and his target.

A thousand years on and we saw the motor car breed the tank and armoured fighting vehicles of all shapes and sizes, the balloon giving way to the aeroplane, which motored along on pistons until they were eventually replaced with jets.

The creed of Technology - further, faster, higher! - ruled then just as it does today.

Now, the "Roman" soldier who stands in that same desert carries more personal firepower than did 1,000 whole Legions of ancient Romans. That's over one million men, all those years ago, easily replaced by a single foot soldier today.

This is just one aspect of force-multiplication, taken to the limits of modern technology, as we currently apply it to armed warfare.

Let one man do what 1,00,000 used to do, but with a better chance of survival. Interestingly, he stills relies on his "chariot" to get around the battlefield, which comes in many forms, from the humble motorcycle all the way up to the exotic helicopter.

But even with all this technology, the modern soldier is still limited by his personal reach. He can only hit what he or his weapons system can see; he can only see as far as the equipment he has will allow him to; and he will only last as long as the rations he carries, until he is resupplied. While his capacity to do his job has been enhanced many hundreds of times by modern technology, he is still dependant on others to multiply his personal force.

Modern man (or woman), is in exactly the same position. No matter how well equipped you are, how much you think you know, how developed your intellect, or how much you have achieved, you will always be limited by the extent of your personal reach. You need other people to multiply your personal power, so you can do things that would normally be beyond your personal limit.

Take the ancient Roman foot soldier and put him in a chariot, and he can wage war on a much wider front, faster, and more refreshed. Give the modern soldier expert intelligence about his enemy, fly him to his killing-zone by helicopter, and resupply him often with material and water, and you effectively extend his reach to wherever you need him to be. Within, of course, the limits of what a single man can achieve in a given period of time.

But give him one more man (or woman) to work with, and suddenly you have an effective force many times greater than just the two people.

Like the charioteer of old, where the two Romans in the cart were able to fight like ten men, coordinating their activities with deadly effect.

The combined skill is always greater than the two individual skills, because the synergy between two people has a force-multiplying effect.

Our modern soldier is superbly equipped, but until he is joined by another, he is but one person. The moment he is force-multiplied, he becomes many people.

Take the element of "Time". While one man sleeps, the other guards. Being able to keep watch during a sleep period gives the soldier a far greater selection of locations to work from. He can comfortably stay hidden closer to the enemy than he would be able to if he were on his own. And having someone guard your back gives you the opportunity to rest and relax, something you would be loath to do on your own.

With two people, you can see twice as much, but at the same time. You can cover ten times the same amount of area, just by spreading yourself apart. You give yourself many, many more options, because the second opinion helps sharpen up your decision making process, and you get a different perspective on a far broader range of subjects.

And then there's the radical advantage you get by suddenly having access to a range of skills that are very different to your own. The other person may well do many of the same things you do, but chances are, he does them completely differently. This gives you a chance to learn by observation, and assess the potential for changing your habits or attitude.

Now many of you will be positive in your own minds that you don't need anyone's help to achieve your life objectives. You look at your role models, and you see strong, resolute people who stand on their own two feet, and take the whole world on straight from the shoulder, no quarter asked or given.

The very essence of their personal power seems to be their individuality, their self-containment, and their self-sufficiency. What you don't see are the legions of support people that stand behind and beside every successful one of them.

People who blend into the background, scurrying around like the army they are, multiplying their leaders' personal power thousands of times over.

The legendary "secretary" who's smarter than her boss.

The magic "switchboard" person who's winning ways make people want to ring you.

The super-efficient "personal assistant" who really knows more about the business than the Chairperson does.

And all the millions of different personalities whose paths we cross, drawing a little from each, without ever realizing it.

All this is, in effect, force-multiplication.

It's one thing to use force-multiplication, but quite another to understand and utilize its potential.

And it involves using all the very best of your people skills, because just as you can't get something for nothing, when you take, you must give back tenfold. The people you relate to and use as an extension of your personal power must always be achieving what they want in life to best give you the benefit of their experience.

If they're not happy, satisfied, motivated, calm, centred, receptive, and giving, then you will never achieve either their potential or your own. In many ways, one of the most bewildering things about working with people is the sheer amount of energy they often seem willing to freely give you in the achievement of your endeavour.

Just as a smile is infectious, and almost impossible to ignore, an air of dedication, the stance of confidence, and the power of a positive attitude do more to motivate people than currency of any kind. People like to be around success, and all the trappings of success. They like to see achievement, both theirs and yours.

And they like to see the worth of their efforts, and be able to judge how they are going relative to what they want to achieve for themselves.

When you choose to use a person as a force-multiplier for your personal power, you are accepting not only one of the great challenges in life, but one of the greatest responsibilities you could ever assume.

You know that personal power comes from purity. Purity comes from inner stance, integrity, intellect, and wisdom.

Thus it is impossible to "use" a person as an extension of yourself in any way but a positive one, and one that is beneficial to both you and the other person. If you try to gain from them selfishly, you will quickly destroy the very thing that you are trying to achieve, for the Universe is very unforgiving, and like all true things, you get back not what you sow, but many times more.

Sow good, harvest a-plenty. Sow bad, reap famine.

Because the learning process is so open-ended, and the intellect so dependent on new energy from discovery and experience, you need to constantly be receptive to everything everyone does around you. In the first pages of this book, the phrase "it's not right, it's not wrong, it's different" was used in relation to how you should view what others do.

This is a key concept, because developing the ability to allow others the right to do things their way, say things their way, and think things their way, is a tolerance not usually found in most people. In fact, the exact opposite is usually true. All too often we selfishly, and wrongly, limit the potential of those around us with preconceptions derived from our own experience or knowledge. We are not receptive to new thoughts and ideas, and we do not welcome input from others that is at odds with what we already feel comfortable with.

In allowing ourselves the luxury of swanning through life with our eyes, ears, and minds so forcefully closed, we deny ourselves the opportunity to learn new things, consider new probabilities, and smell the fresh, powerful scent of heart-quickening stimulation.

So how do you go about making force-multiplication a reality?

It's as easy as granting an interview with your "Self". Settle back, get comfortable, and let the taste buds of your mind consider this conversation :

Self - "Well, then, what is it that you really want out of life?" You think about this question for a while, rolling all the possibilities around in your mind, seeking them for the right flavour, like you would sample a series of fine wines. Finally, you decide.

You - "I want to be healthy. I want to be successful. And I want to make friends, enjoy life, and have all the things I need to do it with."

Self - "I see. Well then, how are you going to do this great thing?" Again, you pause to consider your options, remembering all the different books you have read on the subject, and all the things you have observed in others who seem to have achieved great things with their lives.

You - "I'm going to open my mind to all sorts of different stimulus, I'm going to learn new things, and I'm going to do the things I think are important to me."

Self - "Excellent. Now you have some focus, and some commitment. Your willingness to open up your mind is an exciting possibility - frankly, I've been more than just a little bored with your attitude of late, and I look forward to being refreshed with new input. Now, not wishing to be pedantic, but how exactly do you intend to go about this personal development program you're so interested in?" You pause for the third time, pleased with the compliment paid to you by Self, and encouraged by his (or her) reinforcement of your new found goals and ambition.

How exactly will you go about this project? Good question. Then you have a flash of inspiration, and as if the flood gates of Time have opened up in your mind, you see as clear as the melodious peel of a Church bell the exact starting place for your life quest.

You - "Why, I'm going to use my greatest asset - you - me - my Self - and I'm going to achieve what I set out to do," You shout, excitement and enthusiasm bubbling over.

Self - "Well now, that's all very well. But tell me, what's in it for me? Why should I help You?" You're stunned. You never expected this attitude, or this question, from your Self. You just assumed that when the time came, your Self would be there for You, ready to do whatever it took for You to achieve your life goals.

What to do?

Well, what to do is very much up to you. How you answer this question is about all that you can expect from someone else, were you to ask them to dedicate their lives to your success.

And in truth, why should they?

This, then, is the crucial, pivotal consideration in achieving the benefits of force-multiplication, and being able to draw on the experience and knowledge of others to help you in your life quest.

What's in it for them, and what are you going to do for them, to help them achieve what they desire out of life.

The moment you intuit this, you cement your relationship with your "Self", allowing both sides of your persona to power up, creating the spark that will ignite your intellect, stimulate your mind, and galvanise your attitude towards your ultimate success.

We are all born with an inbuilt sense of "right" and "wrong". As we go through life, we taste both sides of the possibilities, and generally fall into a happy accommodation between the two. Most people enjoy the fruits of "right" most of the time. A few enjoy the superlative fruits of "right" all the time. In being true to yourself, and extending this "truism" to others, you are building the foundations upon which a relationship can be constructed.

And a relationship can only ever be as strong and powerful as the foundations upon which it is built.

Get the basics right - understand what others around you want - and you will soon find that no task is too hard, no question too difficult, and no effort ever spared on your behalf. Just the framing of your life quest in terms that others can easily understand and identify with, will provide you with the majority of your relational foundations.

Solid, empathetic foundations that will allow a bridge to be built, a two-way street between your personality and the personality of the other person or persons.

Now personality means character, identity, ego, individuality, nature, spirit, and soul, so it's a lot more than just the outside shell of the person you are hoping to relate to.

Personality is a many faceted, complex grab-bag of opportunities, all of which demand their own share of attention and stimulus. No one person is a mono-dimensional personality. You need to always be aware that as many divergent forces are working on the intellect of the ones you hope to influence, as there are working on your intellect. And about the same quantity of energy, if not more, needs to be applied to their correct application.

The "people" element is the single most important aspect of the development of your personal power. You can't ever hope to achieve great things with your life until you can easily, repetitively, and consistently build lasting, worthwhile relationships with the people around you.

And no one will ever do something for you for your reasons. They will only ever do them for their reasons. So everything you want to achieve through the force-multiplication process of using other people must always be couched in their terms, not yours.

And that means that you have to take the time and effort to clearly establish exactly what it is that they wish to achieve for themselves, and how you can help them to achieve it!

Technology in itself will only ever let you be more efficient. Just like the bullet is no more than a faster moving, smaller version of the spear, technology merely lets you go faster, further, higher. It can help you to condense the learning process, expedite the execution process, and remove much of the mechanical drudgery from everyday life.

The advent of the computer seemed to promise great leaps in ability and process, but in reality, all it has done is give us a greater reach - a better ability to discover things, and do things by remote control. Understanding still has to be acquired by hard work, and even the fastest, biggest, most expensive computer system in the world is useless unless it is programmed by a human being to do something.

And in many, many situations, the computer has had a pronounced negative affect on the human race. It has taken away a lot of our humanity, and a lot of our drive to achieve things for ourselves. We are only just starting to realise the enormous pitfalls of growing entire generations of information-hungry children on unfiltered, raw television images. Many of the basic skills like reading, arithmetic, and mental process are being subjugated by the desire to push buttons.

Educationists are horrified at the trend towards the "30 second grab" - where knowledge and opinion are only palpable if they come in half a minute, synopsised or paraphrased chunks of dehumanised data.

As with everything in a living, dynamic Universe, eventually a balance will be struck with Technology, and mankind will move on to the next order of development. And who knows, it may well be a computer-based, television screen led advance to the Stars!

But Technology in itself does not make you smarter - you still have to do the work to understand all the information Technology now provides. It will not make you successful - you still have to actually do something with your God-given abilities before you will ever achieve anything. And it will not make you rich - you still have to control it, program it, oil it, and finally, understand it, to ever hope to cope with all the possibilities opened up by the intelligent application of Technology.

It is but a tool, albeit a very powerful and exciting one, that is there to do your bidding. It is an important relationship, but a replaceable one - Technology is there to do your bidding, not you to do it's.

If by magic, every machine in the Universe ceased operation at 5PM today, after the ensuing chaos settled down, the

Human Race would pick itself up, and start all over again, and quickly find a new, different Technology to help advance the development of Mankind.

It may well be vegetable-based, or micro-organic. It may even be single-cell structured, but believe it as you believe in yourself, it will take precious little real time for the innovators, the scholars, the doers amongst us, to get us all started again.

Perhaps you may be one of them?

After all, it's a very simple concept.

Real personal power lies in understanding how to multiply your abilities thousands of times over, by understanding and using the help of those around you, every day of your life.

Real personal power comes from dreaming the possibilities, then making them come true, by dint of hard work and the intelligent use of your intellect.

Now how hard is that?

# THE SHEER POWER OF THE 'ABILITIES

> If there are two characteristics
> that set the really successful person
> apart from everyone else,
> they are "Stickability",
> and "Reliability".
> Without them, you have nothing
> but the empty promise of your potential.

Nothing stands out more sharply than an unfulfilled promise. Nothing hurts more than someone you love and respect demonstrating unreliability. And nothing, but nothing, is more frustrating, than someone who quits before the final siren has sounded. Yet, in today's modern environment of computers and high-tech whizz-bang technology, excuses are manufactured by the millions, often at the expense of the simple effort it would take to get a favourable conclusion.

Loss of face is to be avoided at all costs, and accountability is a thing of the past, as no one cares to assume responsibility for their actions. It's as if we can no longer be blamed for our shortcomings, because of the fear of the potential negative influence it may have on us. The social scientist is King, and all men shall be average, and therefore equal, no matter the real difference in their God-given talents, or in their attitudes.

Take the most recent "serious" War to grace our news media. Post-Gulf War research indicated strongly that the average man in the street believes that Saddam Hussein actually won at America's expense, simply because the Allied war machine stopped short of razing Baghdad, and bombing Hussein into ashes. In a little less than 100 hours of ground-based warfare, the brilliant American-led Allied Armies routed the enemy on every front but one - the Public Relations table.

"One day short!" has been the catch cry in the two years since official hostilities ceased, and the political future of all involved has been essentially negated by what most people believe to be a lack of will on behalf of the President to "see things through" to the bitter end.

History tells us that the call was probably a correct one, as the only thing to come out of a continued action would have been a continuation of the massacre of the Iraq troops and civilians, by a vastly better equipped, and some say, unnecessarily superior force.

But most of us firmly believe that President George Bush lacked the "Stickability" to see the War through to the bitter end. He had the guts to start the conflict, to enlist the help of European and Arab nations, to eventually free an oil-stained Kuwait, while protecting a tense Israel. But when the time came to finish the job, and "take out" Hussein once and for all, he hesitated, and called a halt.

A humane, politically and morally correct decision.

But his credibility has suffered ever since, and his Presidency will be harshly judged by History because of it.

And his failure to be re-elected as the President of the United States is in no small way a direct result of this negative perception held by many of his fellow countrymen.

When you fail to see something through to its conclusion, you, too, are judged harshly. If not by yourself, then by others around you. The pity of it is, that in today's essentially "soft" social environment, the very people who are losing their respect for you, will be the very same ones who offer you a range of excuses to choose from!

This very human trait has been addressed by the study of Human Dynamics, particularly as it is applied to Sports Science.

The concept that has evolved is called "Overloading", and is essentially very simple. For example, if you are a golfer, and have difficulty tuning your different muscles to perform at the same peak level for the four days of a major event, then you are encouraged to create a training program where you do in one day what you would normally do in five.

In effect, you "overload" your normal system with a vastly increased demand, building up your ability to deliver endurance and consistency.

To a champion golfer, this means walking 25,000 metres, (or completing the equivalent aerobic and anerobic exercise), and hitting 350 to 500 golf balls. This is done day in, and day out, until the golfer can hit his one hundredth shot with the same degree of consistency and control at the end of a 1,000 metre sprint, as he hit his first shot of the day with.

By training the body's systems to cope with dramatically much more than will be required under competition conditions, the whole process of completing one professional round becomes many times easier. But does this "overloading" help the golfer to "stick" at it, even when things are not going well for him?

Yes, and no.

In the first instance, performance on demand is a very different requirement to practicing in your own time, and under your own dictated conditions. Perfect practice makes perfect, and in the case of a would-be-champion golfer, once he has the skills, the very best practice is match practice, where he is exposed to the many variables of a real match. Variables such as climate, altitude, the course, the actions of his fellow competitors, and the pressure that he allows to be brought to bear on himself.

But there is a growing body of evidence that the golfer who trains by overloading is not only physically more capable, but mentally more capable. And it is well established now that the mental health, or difference in mental attitude, is all that separates the top fifty golfers in the world on any one day. So if our player knows in his heart and soul that he can hit the ball well no matter how pressured he may be, then there is a very good chance that he will do so.

The negative aspect of this process is that is overlooks the prime ingredient necessary for true "stickability" - commitment. A golfer is committed to finishing, no matter how embarrassing his score, simply by walking out onto the golf course.

You, in your daily lives, are not.

You can elect to practice your life skills by using the science of Overloading, and you will definitely enhance your intellect, your wisdom, and increase your personal power. But without commitment, you will always be able to find an acceptable excuse for not completing things that you start, and you will lack true "Stickability".

Commitment means your ability to execute, affirm, devote, contract, pledge, and entrust your body, mind and soul to the appointed task. Commitment means your ability to see something through no matter what the outcome might be.

Commitment comes from personal discipline - and a heavy desire to be a winner, and not a loser.

At the end of the day, the winner is the only person that doesn't have an excuse. Winners don't need them. Even when they lose by other people's standards, winners still smile, secure in their internalised knowledge that they did their very best under the prevailing circumstances, and that they stuck it out to the bitter end.

In their minds, they did everything possible to deliver on their promise, to utilise their skills to the fullest. They did not quit when the going got tough, and they did not take the easy option - make or accept an excuse for their failure to win.

One of the greatest "minds" to ever live, Albert Einstein, who is still rated as probably the greatest genius of the twentieth century, often said "I am wrong nearly ninety seven percent of the time. It is but the quality of the correct three percent that allows me to do my work, which I judge to be, ofttimes significant".

Ninety seven percent of the time wrong, and only three percent of the time right.

What's your batting average?

Better than Albert's?

What it comes down to is this. If you are going to be a winner, in every sense of the word, then you have to allow yourself to fail at least ninety seven percent of the time. And like all good batters, to get your average up, you have to be at the plate, bat in hand, thousands of times more than those around you, if you are to succeed at what you want to do with your life.

Every good salesman knows that success is all to do with numbers - you call 1,000 prospects, you get 100 responses. From those 100 people you get 10 interviews. Of those 10 prospects you finally get to work your magic on, you will sell four. If you need to sell eight people a week, then you need to start with 2,000 prospects!

Here comes the science of Overloading.

By doing many, many more things, and allowing yourself to fail just like Albert, you will build up your life experience faster, the quality of what you learn from life will be better, and you will be right more often than anyone else simply because you are wrong more often! And when you finally believe that you can see anything through, no matter how tough, even to a bitter end, then you will discover how easy it is to have real "stickability", one of the two most important ingredients in your ultimate success.

Stickability is an attitude, one that is based on knowing what you can do, and what you want to do. Often, you will attempt things that you know you can't probably do. How else are you to learn the necessary things for you to develop your potential? The key factor is that you stick with it, no matter how much it hurts, right up until some conclusion has been reached, right or wrong.

If it's wrong, then regroup, retire, and consider what you have experienced, learn from your mistakes, and move on. Anything you don't understand can be temporarily discarded into one of the two baskets, to await your attention in the future.

If it turns out right, then you will have expanded your potential, empowered your intellect, and cemented the relationship between your ego and your skills, moving the two into closer proximity.

It's interesting to discover just where the saying, "to the bitter end", came from. It will give you heart in your journey, and fire your soul with determination.

In the days of the great sailing vessels, powered by the trade winds, the only reliable way to stop was often as simple as chucking a huge anchor over the bow, and letting massive quantities of chain and rope run out. Eventually, when the anchor took hold, the ship was stopped in its tracks. The skill of a Captain and his crew was judged by the timeliness of this action, and many a wooden wharf around the world bore testimony to a poor sense of timing!

The chain attached to the anchor was always spliced to a "rode", a massive hemp rope, that terminated in what was known as a "bitter end". It got this name because of the wax that was used to fuse the spliced loop into itself, at the point where the hemp terminated. When the sailor doing the splicing pulled the various strands taut, sometimes using his teeth, the taste of the wax was less than joyous, hence the name "bitter end".

If a vessel ran its anchor, chain and rode out to the "bitter end", and didn't achieve its objective, the ensuing crash was usually spectacular, and well worth the effort of clambering down to the jetty to watch the boats dock.

But you can see where the saying came from - the crew had run out everything they had, right to "the bitter end", and still failed in their quest. Better to get there and fail, than to fail and still have rode with its "bitter end" in the chain locker!

Now, everyone likes to be liked. You like your peers to respect you, pay attention to you, and think highly of you and your skills. That's why you promise them so much - you not only want them to be impressed with what you are going to achieve, you want to hold onto their attention, using your promises of great performance to bind them to you.

This is a very human, sometimes socially necessary, trait.

But it can also be the single most destructive habit you can ever develop.

Because the very first time you fail to deliver on one of your promises, you start the cancer of doubt growing in the minds of the very people you most want to impress. Do it again, and you lose that most valuable, bankable, irreplaceable quality called "credibility" - the ability to be taken at your word. You will still be loved, you will still be liked, but you will not be believed, or taken seriously.

And if you lose your credibility, it is almost impossible to get it back, and a deep lurking suspicion often prevents your most ardent believer from actually committing to your promise - because it is often too personally painful for them when you fail to deliver.

They would rather not be hurt again by your failure, than believe you when you say that you will do something.

If your peers, or those around you with whom you share your life, lose their belief in your ability to carry through on your promises, they end up losing respect for you - the very thing you were trying to generate with your promise in the first place!

When you make a commitment, you must do so in the clear knowledge that circumstances might intervene and change your ability to deliver. You must take into account every conceivable possibility, and closely examine how you will deal with each and every one of them. If you genuinely believe that you can deliver, that you have got all the angles covered, then you can offer an unconditional commitment.

But beware!

It is better to offer a conditional statement, and deliver on the promise, than it is to make the promise, and not deliver.

In simple terms, most people would rather you be totally honest with them, and tell them the absolute truth, even if it is hurtful or aggravating, than you tell them something that delivers false hope.

In many instances, when you promise something to somebody, it starts a chain of events based on mutual dependency. Your promise becomes the first link in a long chain of probable events, involving many other, mostly unknown, people. In a sense, your promise of performance is passed on like a baton in a relay race, perfumed and shaped by the different personalities whose hands it passes through.

You fail, and it's like a row of dominos collapsing. Everybody in the link is let down, and made to look foolish by your failure - which they will have no hesitation in passing back to you. Everyone else will condemn you, blaming you for their inability to perform. Their failure will be seen as believing in you - but your failure will be seen as a non-performance.

Do this once, and you might get a second chance. But do it twice, and your credibility will be reduced to a polite "yeah, sure," at the very best.

All you need to do to understand this phenomenon is to place yourself in a similar situation, and imagine that someone you respect and believe in has made a firm promise to you. On the strength of what you have been promised, you have in turn made a promise to someone else, and you eagerly await for the first promise to be executed.

Then boom! No delivery, and you're left standing your ground pointing over your shoulder at the original promiser, feeling hurt and let down. Who do you blame? Do you allow those to whom you promised, to blame you for the failure of the first party?

No.

Which brings us back to the concept of a conditional promise.

When you are relying on other people to do something before you can execute on your promises, you must make it clear that you cannot deliver until this is done. You cannot assume responsibility for events that are outside your control. It is not only stupid and counter-productive to do so, it is unreal, and unworthy of an aware intellect.

The second great 'ability you must develop is depend-ability. There are many aspects to this one word - reliable, sure, accountable, honourable, reputable, secure, solid, trusted, upstanding, dedicated, devoted, faithful, loyal, resolute, true, and authoritative.

The crux of the argument is as simple as this.

Just as you need to be able to trust and rely on other people for the full potential of you personal power to become a reality, so do they need to be able to depend and rely on you.

Again, like so much in life, dependability is an attitude of mind, and as such, is totally controllable by you.

When people depend on you, they are seeking your strength, your wisdom, your compassion, and your intellect. You credibility is at its highest when people depend on you the most. Dependability is a quality that goes beyond mere execution of your normal responsibilities, and the very act of being dependable breeds its own confidence and success.

Positive people attract other positive people, because people group themselves by their attitudes. If you have the attitude of a looser, then you will accumulate negative, down, lost people to your cause.

If you are positive, only the best will turn up, force-multi-plying your personal power. Because energy flows downwards, to get some from the people around you requires that you be highly charged to start with. The negative side of dependency is that if you become dependent on others, you are sacrificing your power to someone else. So you must be the dependable one, the person to whom others look for guidance and stimulation.

If you are accountable for your actions, you are taking responsibility for your life, and you will make of it what you choose. Being accountable means that you need no excuses for failure, and you seek no refuge in self-delusion or public succour. When you stand up, and allow yourself to be identified, you are summoning all the power of others to you, by the very process of taking control of events, and not becoming a victim of them.

People who avoid responsibility, avoid accountability, and need excuses to explain away their failure, are weak and transparent, and lack credibility and respect. You don't like people like this, so why would you expect someone else to like and respect you, if you demonstrated these attributes?

In essence, the difference between a victim and a victor is the tiniest slip in attitude. If you take control, assume the responsibility, stand firm and tall, and orchestrate events around your persona, then the very process of being accountable will empower your intellect.

But if you whimper around, duck the flying accusations, and point the finger at everyone else, you will suffer whatever fate others determine for you. Being a victim is letting everyone else dominate you, control you, and absorb all your energy for their purposes. If you allow this, you are no more than as the fool who fishes at the empty well.

And in the mocking laughter of others, or worse, in the condescending care of a handful of excuses, you will see yourself for what you really are - a lost persona, out of control.

No control, no power.

Great loyalty demands great strength, for often the process of being loyal to a person or a cause forces you to transcend your own common sense. You will often do for others that which you would never contemplate doing for yourself. But loyalty is a great attribute, one that is admired long after the event has passed into history. Respect is a many faceted dimension, and loyalty forms the very core of what respect is generated from. The loyal people in your life stand beside you no matter what - and when your time comes, you must do no less.

Being authoritative is like walking on the edge of a razor blade. On side is fame and fortune, the other, ridicule and distress. Because authority is an assumed poise, one that comes with wisdom and respect. You cannot hope to motivate and prosper with a group of other people unless you have the authority to act. They must give you their permission to take control, and trust you in the execution of that control.

You must give them permission to be critical of your authority, so that you don't overstep your bounds.

The Military have developed authority to a fine art - for a military machine to function, obedience must be immediate and total, or precious lives could be lost by indecision and confusion. A highly structured command process is implemented, with clear and precise lines of communication, layers of responsibility, and ultimately, limits on each individual's authority.

This system can only work while every person agrees to abide by the standing orders. Something which individuals, civilians like you and I, are most unlikely to do.

For us to be able to use our authority, or take an authoritative stance, we must have the voluntary respect and compliance of those around us, or we end up like Captain Blight, adrift on the high seas of mutiny, in a leaking boat of discontent.

Authority should never been confused with strength of purpose, or desire to succeed. True authority comes from knowledge and experience, and leadership qualities that all owe their existence to a positive attitude.

If you are perceived as having "dependability", and you also demonstrate "stickability", and you always make good on your promises, then you will find that those around you automatically give you all the authority you crave or require.

The power of the 'abilities is awesome, just like the potential of your personal power. All it takes is your total commitment to make it all work.

# POLITICIANS ACCOUNTANTS PRIESTS AND LAWYERS RULE OKAY

The school bully was someone
you always hated,
and probably never quite managed
to cope with.
Even now, there are those amongst us
who use their superior education
to terrorise those less informed
than themselves.

The concept of the "Specialist" is as old as mankind. Five thousand years ago, in feudal times, it was the Sage, the Mystic, and the Religious Man who controlled our destiny, with mumbo-jumbo and vague threats that could never be proven. Discipline was maintained by fear, and little or no true respect, other than that afforded to the person because of their exalted position, was forthcoming.

The spirit of the average man was dominated by superstition and fear, and the so called Wise Men took great advantage of this, working their earth magic to protect their status.

The loudest voice, the most informed opinion, and the person who could scare the hapless ordinary man on demand ruled the earth. These people eventually ensconced themselves behind the various seats of power, and used the Kings and

Queens, the Clan Leaders and the Village Chiefs, the Emperors and the Dictators as their means of gaining respectability, and as their protectors and promulgator's.

A King had awesome power over life and death, and the Mystic or Sage had absolute power over the King. Challenge the Mystic, and you challenged the King, and all he stood for.

The Law, as such, was the King's Law, and very much framed to represent and protect the Sage or Mystic who "advised" the King. Rules were framed (as they are today) to advantage the King and his family, and all of humanity was seen as the fodder and the bread basket for the King's every desire.

What was explainable, was the doing of Man. What was unexplainable, was the doing of God (or one of the many hundreds of different Gods thought to be controlling the destiny of the world in those early times).

But the King's Law was the politic form that governed the average life, and the politics of the King were taken as those of the immediate area, or of the land, depending on his area of influence.

Slowly, through the centuries, the King's Law took on a new perspective, and like a triple-headed snake, split into three mutually compatible components, representing the vested interests of three very different types of personality predominant in those times.

The King's Law, Political Law, and Religious Law evolved from the necessity of Kings having to meet, fight, and enjoin with each other. This cross-culturalization of Law and Religion led to many conflicts, as did the vast difference in perceived politics from area to area.

A veritable multitude of discordant Religious Sects grew up like an outbreak of measles, all over the known world during this phase, spreading the corner stones of what would become the five major, dominant forces - Christianity, Buddhism, Confucianism, Islam and Judaism. Each one believed that they were the "one" true Religion, and all the others based on heretical beliefs. In time, even these five were to be split into shards of differing cultures, as strong men fought to retain the essence of their beliefs, while even stronger men fought to change them.

While never officially separated as we know them to be today, the parallel development of Law, Religion, and Politics were all used for the same general purpose - the unashamed domination of the masses, by the born-noble, and the educated and literate few. The Religious Sects saw their role in life as gaining as many converts as possible, to swell their ranks to a size that gave them influence in the corridors of power. The larger they were, the more likely they were able to influence the politics of the day. The stronger their King became, the more likely that their vested interests would be spread throughout the known world.

It was no so much a fight for souls, as a fight for seats!

Many Kings found great advantage in assuming the mantle of these Religious Sects, as it increased their power and their influence far beyond their traditional boundaries, allowing them to dabble in the politics of another King's domain. It also gave them the ability to fuel emotional hatred of the foe, by positioning the chosen "enemy" as non-believers and a threat to their Religion.

History books are filled with the stories of their conquests, wars, and the spread of these cultures by force. Empires came and went, and domination became a fact of everyday life. But the simple truth is that Religion was the focus of conquest for many hundreds of centuries, and the political systems that developed in various cultures owe their existence to the power of the Religious convert.

You only have to read a newspaper now to see that, in this respect, nothing has changed in over seven thousand years! There are at present two hundred and seven wars or areas of embattlement around the globe, and all but two of them involve differences in Religion. Today, the greatest empires to survive History are those controlled by the Holy Roman See, the children of Mohammad, and the students of Confucius.

How this came about, is a matter for Historians, but a quick look into the past will show you that the Chinese Han emperor, Wu Ti, in 136 BC, actually adopted Confucianism as the model for his civil service, and committed the future development of China to the principles of this religion. This situation continued for over 2,000 years. China was the first country to adopt a single religion, and make it part of the persona of the general populace by Law. Others followed, but never on the single scale that China managed to achieve.

For example, during the second century AD, Japan adopted the "Bushido Code" or Code of the Warrior, from the Shinto-Buddhist religion as their focus, and eighteen hundred years later effectively changed the modern world as we know it today, even though their system was partially polluted by the importation of Christianity during the eighteenth century.

The Church of Rome, while not only being the wealthiest single entity on the globe, was also the greatest exponent of exporting both culture and Religion all over the world. Even today, the Roman Catholic Church boasts a significant presence in every country in the world, and still manages to dominate its subjects with fourth century Church Laws.

The Roman Age ushered in the first real signs of the assertion of Law as a supposed force of God, and of course "true" Religion also started to rear its ugly head around that time. Roman Law was the Law of the Senate, an august body of informed people, who were dominated by the emperor, many of whom became dictators. The concept was a simple one, the emperor was the divine messenger of the Gods, who were many, and conveniently different enough to allow him total control over every facet of Roman existence.

And as mankind evolved in this classic era, the continuing fight for supremacy and the Mind of Man started in earnest, as education and literacy spread their tentacles beyond the shallow edges of the Temples and the Government.

Back then, the Temples, which were considered the centre of civilised life, were the repository for the wealthy, the educated, the literate, those that could read and write, and those that could count. Those that could not, held these structures and the people in them in awe, and accepted the mantle of subservience as a matter of fact.

This "civil service" was very much an instrument of the government, the seat of all power, and formed the third level of political influence, as it does to this day.

Predictably, a scribe who kept the books of account was viewed as vastly more important than one who just wrote letters and documents. Even then, keeping an accurate account of who had paid their tithes and levies, and who had not, was a crucial activity. What no one foresaw was the rapid escalation in the power of the men who kept these books of account, and the tragic human consequences that would evolve, as a direct result.

Wars and conquests needed to be funded, and Kings and Emperors alike, liked to live well. That takes money, and as no King or Emperor actually worked at anything other than being "divine", the masses were taxed heavily to support their lifestyle. When a man could give no food, property, or money, he was impressed into the ranks of the Legions as a common soldier.

If they couldn't take your wealth, they took your blood!

And take it they did (and still do) in vast quantities. With no protective system other than distance from the throne, whole families were decimated, generation by generation, for causes little understood, and rarely achieved. And still the accountants of old marked up their columns, using red ink to show a deficit, which, in a terrible way, is symbolic of the blood that was (and still is) spilt in making up any shortfall in the Government's demands.

Very few, if any, questions were asked about this system, as it evolved from within the centre of the political power base, and was taken for granted. The Religious Sects, once they had struck an accommodation with a particular King or Emperor, were virtually powerless to change this system, even if they had wanted to, for to interfere was to risk losing their influence, and their assumed power over the people they dominated.

Thus the tripartite relationship between Religion, Law, and Accounting developed, each mutually dependent on the other for their survival within the political arena.

The talented people who made this system work were very arrogant, and very privileged. They enjoyed better food, better wine, the use of slaves and navvies, lived in better houses, and commanded salaries many hundreds of times greater than the common man could ever hope to achieve.

They were isolated from the pragmatic realities of the day, given that they were responsible for keeping the wheels of privilege and advantage turning smoothly. If they saw poverty and depression, it was passed off as the fault of the common people, for choosing to live such a squalid life. If they saw fervour and discontent, the squashed it like they would kill a cockroach.

Skills were passed from Father to Son, and family dynasties grew up like mushrooms in a wet field. As each "profession" achieved critical mass, they formed Guilds and Societies to propagate their vested interests. Getting into one of these professions from outside the families was almost impossible, marriage being the most popular of the few real alternatives.

Long lines of singular thinking, honed through centuries of stress and fighting for survival evolved, generally speaking, into the four dominant professions we see today - The Accountant, The Lawyer, The Priest, and The Politician.

Interestingly, in the Western world, a recent survey of Politicians from sixty countries showed that an amazing eighty nine percent of all Politicians are either Lawyers or Accountants before they take up politics! So it's not all that hard to see why history seems to repeat itself so often.

As in days of old, once again these Professions are looking after their own vested interests, and making sure that their dynasty survives.

If this seems a harsh judgement, then consider the following.

Accepting that the Politicians are on top of the pile, and given that the Government rules the roost, who is it that determines the size of the Government - the number of Politicians, the number of Government Departments, the number of Civil Servants, and the number of support personnel?

The Politicians do.

Who determines what privileges, rights and payments the Government servants will receive?

The Politicians.

Who determines what the Law of the Land will be - how many Statutes, how many Acts of Parliament or Congress will be promulgated, and how many decrees will be issued?

The Politicians.

And who are the only people qualified, and therefore allowed by Law, to interpret these Laws of the Land for the ordinary folk?

The Lawyers.

Who determines what the Tax rate will be - and what will be paid for, and by whom, and who is exempt, and who is not, and how much the Country will owe, and what the balance of payments (and therefore our standard of living) will be?

The Politicians.

And who is qualified, and therefore the only people allowed by Law to interpret these high-order money matters for us simple people?

The Accountants.

And who, in every level of social endeavour, has the final say as to how and when our souls will or will not be saved, for our eventual trip to eternity?

The Priests.

Every session of Parliament, every sitting of Congress, every conclave of the Law Courts, is opened with a prayer, seeking wisdom and justice. Every Government building is blessed and sanctified, so that those that work in it may do so without fear of ghosts, or evil spirits. Even in today's high-tech environment, the trilogy of power is firmly held by the Lawyers, Accountants, and Priests, who support the entire political system, and the Politicians within it.

In 1992, the Federal Tax Act was two hundred and forty five thousand pages thick, bound in four hundred and ninety volumes, and subject to a further one hundred and twenty six thousand pages of amendments!

Does this seem reasonable? Must the Tax Act, which, in effect, determines how well we each will live, need to be so complicated that millions of man hours are required just to understand it?

Is it reasonable for the average man to feel (and this is well documented by volumes and volumes of independent research) that he is utterly powerless to change this situation?

And is it reasonable for someone to go from the cradle to the grave, never feeling in control of their own lives, or their destiny? Simply because they have a Government that is dedicated to its own survival, at the expense of the ordinary man?

What does any of this have to do with someone seeking the path to developing their personal power?

Everything, and nothing.

For there is much to learn from the Politicians, Lawyers, Priests and Accountants, and their mysterious, sometimes dubious, ways.

Like the lessons of the Fox, it is not necessarily wrong that they should take advantage of their situation, it is often the way in which they do it that is of prime importance to us.


No one liked the school bully, because he took advantage of your immaturity, your lack of awareness, your lack of physical development, and your lack of self-esteem. He embarrassed you. He dominated you simply by terrorising you into submission, mostly by what he threatened to do to you, rarely by what he actually did to you.

He used your ignorance and fear as a weapon, subjugating your will, and trampling your spirit. He left you feeling confused and empty, but somehow dependant. The very process he put you through so lowered your self-esteem, he actually created a mild form of dependency in your mind, almost as if you weren't worth much if he wasn't bothering to bully you.

This phenomenon has been seen many times in recent years, in victims of highjacks and kidnappings. The victims seem to bond with their abductors, generating strong feelings of comradeship, even though they are often faced with losing their lives in the process! It is believed that the fear level gets so high during these tragic escapades, that when a person realises that they may survive, their gratitude towards their terrorist captors is overwhelming, creating the relationship that is perceived as dependency.

And it is this dependency that you, as a true seeker of personal power, must come to grips with. Just like in school days, it is your ignorance and your fear of the unknown that will hold you hostage, and allow you be dominated by a Lawyer, Priest, Accountant, or Politician.

Let's take them one by one.

A good Lawyer is someone who knows where to find the Law, not necessarily one who practices it.

But every text, case study, judgement, proclamation, judgement and verdict is always written in a language that is only interpretable by "one who knows". In this way, the Law Profession is able to propagate itself. By what it does, and how it does it, it guarantees its very own survival.

The majority of Western Law is based on precedence, or that which has gone on, and been adjudged, before.

In dealing with a situation that requires a Lawyer, you must understand the vested interest. It is not with you, or with your particular case. It is about keeping the Profession in the good light it thinks it presently enjoys, and in keeping you in the dark for as long as is acceptable.

Much to do with Lawyers is about "opinion", and all too often opinions differ with every new personality involved in the process. Television has made a science out of the presentation of Law, and the truth is, unfortunately, the performance is almost always more important than the facts.

Short cases earn small fees. Lawyers are paid by the hour, by the phone call, by the diary entry, by the meeting, and by the opening of a book. Win, lose, or draw, you pay. And in all but the very simplest of cases, you will have very little to judge your progress by, or the quality of the service you are receiving, or the value of your investment.

In the first instance, the very best way to deal with this situation is not to have to involve Lawyers at all! But sometimes, this is not practical, or in your best interests. If you have to use a Lawyer, then you have to have control over the process. You must document your case, your questions, your opinions, and your objectives. You must get the Lawyer to resolve your issue only along the lines of your brief. And you must learn to approach the Lawyer as an equal, and meet them on common ground.

They don't understand the concept of customer service, and they are scared by anything that appears to be outside their immediate area of control. For you to control them, you must be in control of yourself, and your situation. You must have the facts, and expectations that are reasonable. And you must always ask for reference material from similar cases, so that you can better understand your true position.

You must never be in a position of dependency, where they are in control of your future. To do that, is to allow the school bully to bluff you yet again.

Dealing with a Priest is different. Here you are in an excellent position to meet them on equal terms, because every Religion has its own guide book - The Bible, the Koran, and such like. Your opinion is worth the intensity of your study. Whatever you put into learning about your chosen (or inherited) Religion, will only further your cause, and enlighten your life. Spiritual health is every bit as important as physical and mental health. Some say more so.

Knowledge is power. Understanding is power. Fear is banished by knowledge and understanding. You only fear what you don't know, so open the pages, and soak up the context of your relationship with your God.

Priest's acknowledge and respect people who know their own minds, are secure in their own beliefs, and take the time and energy to learn what is important to them. Of all the Professions, they are the most Intune with the common man, but they still have a time honoured tradition of siding with the King to protect their Sect, when push comes to shove.

Again, understand the vested interest. It is most unlikely that you will ever be a real threat to a Priest or his Church, but should you be, you can expect the wrath of the most devastating political and military machine on earth to descend on your head with all the force of Heaven and Hell.

After all, that's the business they are in.

Many of today's Accountants should still be kept in their temples, counting dinars and goats teeth. Few, if any, ever contribute to the welfare of mankind, or push the boundaries of knowledge beyond their own limited horizon. They are often referred to as "bean counters", and judging by many that you meet, this would appear to be a perfectly adequate description.

Yet today is the era of the Accountant, as the world scrambles for the magic saviour called "the bottom line". People and loyalty are seconded to the all-important dollar, as company after company sheds staff in an effort to return profits.

It was the Accountants who developed the skills necessary to purchase companies, sell off their assets for more than their cost price, sack all their staff, then close them down, taking the ensuing loss into account, to the direct benefit of their next wealth-generating scheme. It was the very same Accountants who decided that farmers should be turned off their land, and their properties sold out from under them, reducing genera-tions of love and toil to a single red entry in a dusty book of life.

Unfortunately, with the Tax Act - the gigantic mishmash of numerical numbnuts that it is - you need an Accountant to make sure you have complied with the most recent interpretation. So, once again, you find yourself in the position where if you are not properly prepared, and in control, you will be dependent on someone that does not have your best interests as his vested interest.

Prepare, and prepare well. Leave nothing to chance. Document everything, and follow the Law to the absolute letter. Take a long-term view, and plan for the future, and be sure that the commercial or personal advice you receive is something that you can live with morally, ethically, and most importantly, spiritually.

Cutting corners with money destroys people. Money in itself is not real wealth. It is what you do with it that gives you wealth and happiness. Money is just little bits of paper, plas-tic, and metal that you trade to others for goods and services. Money is but a way of measuring your progress and worth by other's standards.

The happiest man you will ever meet will have very little money, but much wealth. He will be wealthy with love, wealthy with companionship, and wealthy with health and success. And his smile will be infectious.

The Accountant mentality, unfortunately, is what often drives us to pursue money at all costs. To become greedy, addicted, and selfish. The need to have it, see it, touch it, and been seen to have it, can become overpowering influences in our lives.

But there is one attribute of the Accountant that gives us hope for our future as a united people. And that is their ability to cope with a dichotomous situation that baffles many, and we should learn from it.

You see, in accounting terms, a debit or a credit can be posted to either side of the ledger, depending on its category. This means, in very simple terms, that something that is to be deducted from a sum, can have a positive value. In your perspective, then, it is possible to be going through a negative experience, but with a positive outcome.

Who said accounting was easy to understand?

But what you must understand about Accountants is that, by profession, they are literal, numerate, and often pedantic. They will not usually share your great vision, your energy, or your wonder at all things possible. They like certainty, money in the bank, and creativity limited to selecting the correct restaurant for lunch.

Understand this, and they can never put you in a position where you might become dependent on them, to the detriment of your personal power.

And power is what Politicians are all about. Lots and lots of it. But not the type of power you seek.

Politicians crave dominance, position, authority, and influence, at the expense of the common man.

Politicians have taken the art of compromise to a high-order science, in their frantic race to manipulate everything around them.

And Politicians have single-handedly destroyed the concept of representation and fairness in the community, in their ruthless pursuit of Irresistible force. They speak like Gods, act like Gods, condescend like Gods, and command like Gods. They live in isolation, happy to be segmented from the reality of normal life, and their sole contribution to the welfare of their constituents is that they always claim to be pushing their cause.

It is often said that we, the people, get the Politicians we deserve. If that is true, then we are surely being punished for the sins of our fathers. But the reality is, that many of today's Politicians were good people before they were corrupted by the system.

Now, companies don't do things, people do. Parliaments are huge buildings, that are dormant and hollow until people give them life with their presence. So what is it that goes so tragically wrong in the corridors of power?

Absolute power corrupts, absolutely.

Power - force, authority, control, influence, leverage, prestige, command, rule, might, mastery - is like a drug. The wielders of power become addicted to what they have, and they don't want to let it go. It is the greatest ego trip in the world, sitting on top of a huge pile of humanity, deciding how they will live, and how they will die. It is the very same force that the Kings of old used so poorly. And Politicians, like the Kings and Emperors before them, have no greater God-given gift or ability to deal with this than you do.

Remember, most Politicians are Lawyers and Accountants before they become Politicians. And you now understand a little about both those Professions. So it is logical to assume that many of the characteristics of the Lawyer and the Accountant are present in the Politician.

Language used like a subterfuge, to disguise what is really going on. Proceedings always under the privilege of Parliament or Congress, so the ordinary person has no legal redress against what might be said. Self-appointed committees of review, who's reports are tabled, then consigned into the dusty tombs of the archives. Statutes of limitation on what is revealed to the public, and when it might be. All in all, what we have is close to the perfect form of self-control, and self-containment.

If you aren't part of the system, then you don't "need to know". And unless you are prepared to marry a Politician's son or daughter, there's almost no way in for the ordinary person. Just like the privileged families from the Temples of old, in classic times.

We have all seen a grown, mature man, literally turn grey in four short years, under the weight of responsibility that goes with the top job in the land. But grey hair doesn't necessarily mean wisdom, and often it is the stress and pressure caused by ignorance and confusion that ages them, not the job. That, and the pressure to compromise almost everything they believe in, often the very things that got them elected in the first place.

Understand this, and you will get a beneficial perspective on the development of your personal power. Without it, should you succeed in your life quest, you will quickly dissipate your real power, without ever knowing how or why you did so, and then your quest will have been for nothing.

# SLEEP ON IT

Sometimes it seems that your problems
are so great and so many,
the sheer weight of them threatens
to swamp you.
Most of all, what you need
is a sure fire way to deal with them,
even with your eyes closed.

As you move along your chosen path, you have to make millions and millions of decisions. Rational, and sometimes, irrational behaviour, determines the how, what, when, why's of our life, as we exercise our God-given power that we are all born with, to choose our destiny. Some decisions come hard, and some are made easily, almost automatically, and some of the time you are not even aware of having made them.

But the ones that stand us up, and back us into a corner, are the demons you have to learn to cope with, if you are to fully realise your personal power.

Indecision kills, action thrills.

Like a blocked artery that denies the heart precious blood, when you choke on a hard or difficult decision, you deny your intellect the energy it needs to resolve the issue for you.

And the amazing thing is, the very split second you consciously or unconsciously decided to do something, the paralysing block is removed, the weight of the world lifts from your shoulders, and you feel free!

In achieving a goal, or objective, just as in resolving a problem, or making a decision, there is always an apparent barrier. Sometimes it's a little one, and of no real consequence. And sometimes it's so apparently huge, it threatens to overwhelm you before you can resolve it.

But apparent barriers are always emotional, never rational. Apparent barriers are things you concoct in your heart and your mind, like dubious pictures from a fright show. And because you believe in them so much, you empower them, making them seem real, and giving them a life they don't deserve.

These apparent barriers always, but always, are the result of a practical problem. But it is the sheer strength of your emotional reaction to these practical problems that is the barrier you have to deal with - not the practical problem itself. Practical problems are always resolved practically. Emotional problems need recognition, and attitudinal change, for them to be overcome.

Remember the two baskets of knowledge used by the scholars of old? One held all that was understood about the known world, and the other held all that was fear, superstition, magic, acts of the devil, and things just too plain confusing to understand. This second basket is the one that tended to draw scholars to it, like a flame draws a moth. Sheer curiosity, man's thirst for knowledge, and the wonderment of the unexplained fired the imagination, and fuelled the seekers of truth and wisdom to the point where they willingly risked death by all manner of painful methods, just to hold, for a fleeting second, the power of discovery in their hands.

One by one, they peeled back the many layers of the onion, revealing the secrets of the Universe that we now take so much for granted.

Many, many times, they were faced with seemingly impossible situations, simply because they were confronted with something that was beyond their experience. They had no frame of reference for what they were observing or experiencing. To get it, they had to try things, experiment, test the water, as it were. And gradually, as they learned from experience, they built up a body of knowledge that allowed them to move deeper and deeper into the realm of the unknown.

Their experience was essentially a solitary one, as they lacked computers, satellites, telephones, newspapers, magazines, mail, or any other form of mass communication, to share their discoveries, and learn from the mistakes and successes of others. What they learned, and lived to talk about, tended to stay within the immediate district, at least for a few hundred years or so. Many scholars could be working on the same problem, all within two hundred leagues, and never know about each other. They had to face down their own demons on their own, and hope that at the end of it all, they would still be alive to move on to the next challenging, unsolved mystery.

Then, as now, resistance forced change.

Something that needed explaining, resisted the will of man, forced man to change his attitude towards the situation, to go about solving the apparent problem. Not to do so was to risk being swallowed by the demons of fear and ignorance!

They soon discovered that fear was directly proportional to lack of knowledge. The more they learned about something, the less fearful it became. The more they understood the forces of the Universe, the more unlikely they were to be spooked when something inexplicable occurred. As their reference base grew, so did their ability to deal with the unknown.

Today, in the closing stages of the twentieth century, fear is still the precursor of ignorance. It is what you don't know or understand that creates the emotional barrier that robs your intellect of its power.

The practical situation, the cause of the emotional barrier, because it is not well understood, causes you to resist - and you fear the situation all the more for its apparent overwhelming potential - "How the hell can I ever do (understand, cope with) that!" Emotionally, you boil over to the point that you convince yourself that what you believe is true, and an seemingly unshakable, apparent barrier solidifies to the point of paralysis.

What to do?

Solving problems is essentially easy. Just like the scholars of old, you have to recognise the two baskets, and apportion your analysis of the problem to each of them. What you know, can safely reside in one, what you do not know must be firmly placed in the second. The moment you do this, you have removed a major portion of the resistance that faces you, because you have started a process that will eventually allow you to solve the problem, no matter what it is, or how big it may seem.

Once what you don't understand is clearly in the second basket, you can decide how to attack it. What do you need to know, learn, establish, find out, or further analyse, to move the contents into the other basket, the one that holds what you are comfortable with? While this may seem to be a very holistic way of going about making decisions, it is actually quite practical, and logical.

Like the scholars of old, all you are doing is breaking the apparent problem down into small, easily coped with component parts, each of a size that you can easily and rapidly deal with. You are being quintessentially pragmatic and logical in your approach, winding your emotions back to a level where you can maximise your stimulation, or arousal, positively, rather than let it freeze your intellect with fear.

Since the advent of the writing instrument, listing down all you know about something has been a recognised method for opening up a solution to a problem. Likewise, if you describe in the fullest detail what you think the problem is, then list everything you can think of alongside it, you will often find that a solution, or many solutions, suddenly appear in your mind, each one every bit as strong and believable as your first apparent emotional barrier was.

And as wise man once said, "A problem well defined, is half solved".

Of course, not all problems need to be attacked with the fullest force of your intellect. Problems, like ant bites, come in many sizes, and many intensities of potential pain. And surprisingly enough, thousands of these problems often seem to solve themselves, given the time to do so.

Which introduces a critical aspect of making a decision.

Timeliness.

You already know that pressure is a force that you apply to yourself, or, through your attitude, allow others to place on you. Pressure goes hand in hand with emotional paralysis, and is a by-product, or an instigator, of fear. But a lack of perceived time within which to solve your problem will apply more pressure to you than any lack of knowledge, because the human existence, unlike any other on earth, is dominated by time.

You never have enough of it. It is always passing you by. And as every year goes past, it seems that it goes by faster.

But "time", or an apparent lack of it, is not the enemy. It is simply the focussing mechanism that allows us to achieve things we would not normally be able to do. It is no more a threat than ignorance, and in many ways is vastly more beneficial to your process than any other consideration. "Time" forces you to plan your attack on your problem, prioritise your actions, and set deadlines for your achievement. Without time, you could wander aimlessly through your problem, never feeling the need to reach a conclusion, and move on to the next objective, and fritter away the most precious of all life's commodities.

In every organisation where there is never enough time to execute something the way it should be, it always turns out that, as if by magic, there's suddenly enough time to do it twice!

The subject of "time" is covered in a dedicated chapter, and you will do well to spend some quality "time" there. At this point, what is of upmost importance is that you clearly understand that "time" is no more or no less than what you do with it.

You control "time", not "time" controls you.

"Time" just is, continuously, a constantly moving part of the space-time continuum.

What you do and achieve in your "time" is what counts, not how much time passes, or is left to you. Just as the process of learning is where the value comes from, not the actual knowledge acquired, so is it that your use of time is what determines your level of personal power.

And how well you make your decisions will be reflected in how much time you have at your disposal. The faster you make your decisions, and the greater the quality of them, the more time you will have for your quest. It is axiomatic that just when you need time the most, there isn't any, and when you have heaps of it, you can't think of anything to do!

Yet, if you carefully observe your personal role-model, or someone you respect as being successful with their life, it is a safe bet to say that he or she always seems to have all the time in the world for anything they choose to do. And, perhaps, they always seem to do things effortlessly, as if working to some secret plan or agenda. It's almost as if they are so in control of their "time", that it does their every bidding.

What you observe is true. They are in control of their "time", and it is doing their bidding. To understand how, read the chapter titled, "Time, More or Less".

Decisions that seem to make themselves without any conscious effort, are worthy of close examination. For a decision to be made, you need to have the necessary frame of reference; the knowledge; the ability to perceive the real issue; and the desire to overcome any perceived barrier that your emotions may have erected.

To achieve all these aspects without conscious effort would suggest that you always were capable of making this particular decision, but just didn't see the need to do it at that time. Yet another example of timeliness.

If you don't have to do something right now, then don't.

If you don't have to make a particular decision right now, at this specific point in time, then don't. Not because it's not necessary, but because there may be nothing to be gained from it, at this time. Often, not understanding this point is what accelerates the apparent pressure you feel, associated with the decision you think you have to make.

Just as you can't do someone else's work for them, you can't make their decisions. Just as they can't make yours. Help and advise, yes. Act as a sounding board for your ideas, absolutely. But do the work for you, never.

Imagine a very long railway line, stretching far into the depths of your imagination. Visualise lots of branch lines, each setting off in a different direction, via their own set of points. Somewhere down the track, most, but not all, of these branch lines come back to the main line, blending into the original track. Thus we have a picture of a long, finite route, with many different ways to get to the conclusion. Some will be direct, others circuitous, still others demanding a back-track, as they end abruptly in a dead-end.

Your life quest is to reach the end of the track, with as few diversions as possible. Because each branch line sends you off into unknown territory, for an unknown quantity of energy and time, you must never be in a position where you end up on a line that you didn't intend.

This is what the decision making process is like. If you are focussed, and prepared, have a broad base of understanding, and consequently a wide frame of reference, you won't be switched off to an unwanted side track by unforeseen events. But you will always be free to choose your own route, and go off and explore the mysteries of life whenever you choose to, in whichever direction best suits your purpose.

And you will always seem to have all the time in the world to do it in.

The very process of being prepared, focussed, and informed, gives you the freedom to selectively choose which route you will take to reach the end of the track, and what time frame you will do it in. At all times, you are in control, steadily sampling the fruits of life, enjoying the limitless expansion knowledge and experience provides, fuelled by your vision and your personal power.

The unconscious decision is a very important one, because it is being made by that part of you which knows you best. The deep well of your soul has an inescapable imprint of your destiny, and will do all that it can to see that your triumph in your quest. The biggest single problem is that all too often, you consciously interfere in its activity, and try to take over the process, and force the issue.

It's just like grabbing a handful of mercury, that mysterious liquid metal that finds its way into all sorts of useful devices. The tighter you squeeze, the more that falls out. The gentler you cradle it, the longer you can control it.

Reality, perception, experience, knowledge, wisdom, and understanding all fuel the inner self, the unconscious side of the mind. Just as you are the sum total of all your experience, so is your intellect the sum total of all that you are. To really reach its peak, and motivate you efficiently, it must be freed up to operate on its own, free from interference, filtering, and presumption.

You can construct any reality you wish, and believe it to be the truth. Believe it hard enough, and it will become the truth, because you will make it happen that way, consciously and unconsciously. Such is the power of your mind. The greatest power you will ever develop is your ability to visualise events and objectives, with a clarity that makes them become a reality for you.

Just as you manufacture an emotional barrier because of a perceived practical problem, so can you manufacture a solution to the problem, simply by letting your mind work on it, unfettered by your assumptions or your fears. The biggest, strongest, most physically perfect human being is still only as powerful as his (or her) intellect allows him to be. The power you hold within you is your key to the Universe.

Intuition is often thought of as the Voice of God. We know it as a hunch, an instinct, a premonition, a sense or awareness, a feeling, or a subconscious direction from our intellect. Many times, you cannot adequately explain where your hunch of feeling came from, or what prompted it in the first place. And the more you chase it, the further it seems to go away. It is, because it is, and that concept in itself is a difficult one for a modern person to sometimes cope with.

Out with those two baskets of knowledge again!.

But whatever it may be in reality, your intuition is fuelled by your overall experience. Instinctively, you always do what seems right to you, without thinking about it. Your persona determines your inner stance, and your inner stance frees up your intellect to work for you, unconsciously. This is what intuition really is.

It is your unconscious mind telling you, as firmly as it can while you are awake, what it thinks you should do, or what it thinks the correct course of action should be.

In the sealed section of Part 2 of this handbook, you'll find a wealth of knowledge concerning your mind, and how it works, and how you can take advantage of it. The section is sealed because, like the proverbial can of worms, once you let this type of information out, you'll never be the same person again!

A recurring point that has been made in various ways during this brief look into "time", is your ability to integrate several different attitudes and practicalities into a frame of reference, making it all that much the easier for your decision-making ability to be empowered. There is one, magical, four letter word that utterly sums this process up - it is, in fact, a literal truth, and you now know how rare they are!

The word is "PLAN".

Go back to the railway in your mind, and view it as if from a helicopter. Suddenly you can see all the branch lines that end in disaster. The most interesting of the possibilities that you wish to experience on your life path suddenly become clear to you, and as you land the helicopter, a plan forms in your mind, a simple order of potential experience.

In other words, you selectively decide which branch lines you will go down, and in what order. You eliminate all the branch lines you don't need, condensing the task into a finite, easier to manage, process. The basis of your plan is a series of decisions that shapes your reality - you have decided where you will go, and when.

Now, should something untoward happen, you have a frame of reference against which you can judge the necessity to change your plan, instead of being in the fickle, calloused hands of chance.

A life plan can be as simple as one strong, vibrant, dedicated picture in your mind, of what it is that you most want to be. Believe in it enough, empower it, and it will come true. You will become what you see yourself as.

Millions of excellent words have been committed to this subject, and they are all worth pursuing.

A life plan can be as complex as a blow-by-blow outline of what you intend to achieve for yourself, detailed to such an extent that you have an outline for every day!

Irrespective of the size, or the content, it is your belief in the plan that will make it work, not the plan itself. However, the distinct advantage of having a plan is that decisions will be much easier for you to make, because you will have a powerful frame of reference against which you can judge what it is you need to do.

Planning is a process of assembling facts and fancies into a usable form, with a time application. Because it is a process, you learn and gain great value from it. The plan that results in this process is like anything else in this world, it is only of value if it is executed. Like your abilities, a plan in itself is worth nothing until you do something with it.

Another aspect of the decision making process is a phenomenon called "expectation". When you make decisions, you create an expectation of something being achieved, or executed. Your intellect is fuelled by the possibilities of something being done, from which you will derive either a practical or emotional benefit. Expectation runs the highest when the chances of success are the strongest.

But the opposite is also true, whenever you let yourself become blocked by an emotional barrier, and crippled by your inability to make a decision. The pressure that you take upon yourself mounts, warps your vision, pollutes your mind, robs your intellect of its ability to solve the issue, and you start to worry about the consequences. Your inactivity, and the probable consequences of the decision merge into one amorphous mass of concern, adding even more pressure.

Thus a vicious cycle is created, usually far greater in apparent scope and worth than is the original decision. Sadly, experience shows that better than 98% of everything you actively worry about under these strenuous circumstances never comes true, so it would seem to be a tragic waste of your talents to let yourself get into this situation.

The added disaster of this negative situation is that in spending your life-time worrying needlessly about the 98% that never happens, you miss the glory of the 2% that does!

One soothing thought - if you genuinely reach a point where it seems impossible that you can resolve a decision, try creating a simulation of the problem, and experiment with different solutions. In this way, before you commit to a particular line of thinking or direction, you can taste a whole world of possibilities, just by playing the "what-if?" game.

The very next time you are faced with this situation, and it does indeed seem to be a seemingly impossible decision to make, create your simulation. And then sleep on it. You may well find, that as the first golden rays of the new day fight their way into your consciousness, the decision has made itself, or possibly rearranged itself into a different shape - one that is more approachable, and easier to deal with.

The key to decision-making is doing something. Always. It's that simple.

# THE IRRESISTIBLE LURE
# OF THE COMMON MIND

People tend to group themselves
by their attitudes.
Just like gravity,
whose Irresistible force keeps
us all in our rightful place,
attitude tends to determine
the kind of people we mix with.

In 1969 mankind broke free of the shackles of gravity and two unique men stood on the moon. They were still affected by it, but only one sixth as forcefully as they has experienced just days before back home on planet Earth. The event will long be remembered for Neil Armstrong's "....small step for man, giant leap for mankind..." speech, as it should be. But on that day, nearly a quarter of a century ago, this one extraordinary event linked billions of people from all countries, races, and religions, via the television screen, and the radio speaker.

One single human event linked every mind, with one common desire. To see the first steps to the Stars etched into the dust bowl known as "The Sea of Tranquillity".

Every shop-front that had a TV set drew huge crowds of expectant watchers. Companies and boardrooms around the world stopped in their tracks, and listened and watched as the first true space explorers raised the silver grey dust of the Moon, leaving rippled footsteps as a permanent record of their achievement.

A single, imaginative, unbelievably challenging act of man banished the cares and differences of the whole world, for approximately 47 minutes.

What drew all these vastly different cultures together in awe was the magic of the conquest of space. The fact that a man was standing on the moon, something that was in plain sight most nights, so tantalizing close, yet so far away, and that they were seeing it live, as it happened (albeit a few seconds late, due to the route the transmissions had to take to get back to Earth, and the distance between the Earth and the moon), snapped into sharp focus the possibilities yet to be explored.

In a sense, all the comic books, and all the fantasy and fiction books came to life in one glorious moment of discovery, and the golden age of science fiction became the shimmering age of science fact.

For most of us, the possibilities of travelling freely in space will remain but a dream, sometimes satisfied by either a virtual reality experience, a good movie, or a better book. But for others, the ones in training (or soon to be) for Space Station Discovery, these early, somewhat clumsy steps will lead to voyages to the Stars, and the ever patient Galaxies beyond.

Mankind and space belong together, just as our ancestors belonged to the sea. For true discovery always involves a journey of uncertainty, with seemingly miserable practicable rewards, but exciting and stimulating intellectual ones.

While what the first steps of space exploration achieved will quickly pass into history, as our knowledge expands, the feeling that they generated is something you can discover every day of your life. That great sense of accomplishment, of having taken part (no matter how small, insignificant or remote) in something so vast and imaginative, something that is very much out of the ordinary scope of your daily existence.

The feeling is huge, it can well up tears in your eyes, and it can choke you with emotion. And if it is based on a vertical experience, it will empower you to greater things.

A close examination of this phenomenon shows us that the positive structure of accomplishment generates huge energy quanta, which is always reflected in your attitude, and thus in your inner and outer stance. Other people see this in you, and either are attracted to you, or repelled by you, depending on their attitude.

From early school days, you know that positives (+ve) repel each other, as do negatives (-ve), just like the poles of a magnet. Unlike poles attract. This is the exact opposite with attitude, or inner stance, where positive attracts positive, and negative attracts either negative, or nothing. Unlike attitudes usually settle uncomfortably somewhere in the straight-jackets of conformity or compromise.

The expansionist inclination of the mind is responsible for this, as intellect is both fuelled and empowered by fertilisation, stimulation, association, intangibles, perspectives, conceptions, mystery and magic, all of which are best encountered in strong relationships with other people. Every place you go, there is always one person who is highly visible, and has a large group of people surrounding them, while another person, far less intrusive, haunts the shadows, with a smaller but more intense audience.

The former is the "legend in his own lifetime" style of achiever, who usually draws shallow, easily swayed people to him, who fuel his ego, but never his intellect. His (or her) role is to feed off the power of others, sucking your self-esteem and self-worth from you, to prove his assumed superiority. The smarter they are, the dumber you appear to be, for there can only ever be one hero in their sphere of influence.

The other achiever, the one who unassumingly finds themselves ensconced in an interesting group, tends to be the more serious of us, constantly challenging the precepts and norms of society, always seeking stimulation for his intellect. The people who surround him (or her) are there to learn, and to teach, and to share, and to grow in each other's presence.

When you experience a meeting or close encounter with a "legend" you are left breathless, but empty. You go away with a vague feeling of uneasiness, as if you left something behind, but you can't remember what.

You did.

You left behind some of your self-respect, because the shallowness and vacuousness of the encounter caused you to mentally (if not verbally) diminish the worth and outer stance of the focus of your attention, the "legend". And in losing respect for someone, you forfeit a small measure of respect for yourself.

The contrary is true of the second person. Because you are there to share, to learn, and to be stimulated, you come away with a warm, positive feeling that you have grown in both personal stature and intellect.

It isn't just personal contacts that can fuel this enormously powerful feeling in you. Paintings, books, films, stories, poetry, meditation, visualisation, experimentation, simulation, and commitment all have the power to juice your intellect.

And all this is driven by one clear picture - the picture you have of yourself, of who you are, and what you stand for. It is the clarity of this picture that draws others to you, in direct contradiction of the laws of physics.

If this wasn't so, then the biggest puzzle of the Universe would have no foundation - the fact that, in many cases, two people who seem to be diametrically opposed as personalities, get together in a close relationship. A union that, when viewed from the outside, seems an impossible one.

Yet these relationships exist, and in the majority, not the minority.

The dynamics at work are easy to visualise - what is linking these people together is a common, shared, mutually enjoyable attitude, that may well not be reflected in their personalities when viewed as singletons. In essence, what is attracting the other person is the invisible, internalised, unchangeable "you", that lurks deep in the soul of every person.

It has been said that true love is the ability to care, feel and do something for someone else at the expense of yourself. If this is true, then true understanding is the ability to feel, hear, and comprehend someone else at the expense of your own belief system and ego. Understanding that it's not necessarily right, it's not necessarily wrong, it's just different!

In other words, by your attitude, you allow the other person to be who and what they think they are, without challenge, or fear of failure.

The greatest gift you ever give another person is permission to speak. The next greatest gift is the permission to fail. And the overriding greatest gift is to allow them to be themselves, in an environment that is conducive to their growth as a person.

Respect and love are often confused as being the same thing, and it is easy to see where these two intense feelings can cross over and merge. But respect, even out of love, is something you earn, usually by performance. When you respect someone, you are, in effect, saying that you would consider seriously anything they had to say. Or you may be referring to their achievements, that you are marvelling at in contrast to your own.

Love is very different. Love is an all-consuming, passionate, totally encompassing feeling that is so strong you could literally kill for it. (And sadly, many do.) Love is what drives common men to great heights, and great men to their collective knees. Doing something for someone else, freely, unreservedly, and with all your heart and soul is the most powerful thing you can ever achieve as an individual.

But true love requires great distance, and distance requires confidence, trust, respect, and perspective. "Absence makes the heart grow fonder" is an old adage, not well understood. But those of you who have really experienced true love will understand the totality of this most powerful feeling, and what it means to be able to physically leave the people concerned for long periods of time.

Love is the one true, great, horizontal experience, right after belief in yourself. Because for you to be able to love someone with all your heart, all your soul, and all your might, you must first truly love yourself, unreservedly, and unashamedly.

And that is not an easy thing to do.

If you start with respect, then you start with the building blocks of a good relationship. If you start in awe, then you will flounder on the inevitable ego that is predominant in such a situation.

And awe is not respect, and respect is not necessarily a powerful, or even correct motivation, to do something. Respect should be born out of observation and regard of facts, not speculation or rumour. All too often we find ourselves being led down the path of frivolous, time-wasting, energy-sapping emotional stimulus, that has no foundation in truth. Only to find that at the end of it all, we are left empty, unsatisfied, unfulfilled, and emotionally drained.

When you stand in awe of someone, you are giving them some of your power. You are allowing, simply by your deferential attitude, your energy to flow towards them. You also weaken your ability to observe and learn from them. Your vision is coloured by your expectations, and you filter your input by what you condition yourself to believe.

The first man on the Moon, Neil Armstrong, was not ten feet tall; he didn't have a multitude of degrees and honours; and he didn't have super-human ability. What he did have was a burning desire to achieve his goal - to be the first man to stand on the Moon - and he did the work that was demanded of him at that time to achieve that objective better than anyone else on the Apollo Program.

He was also quite short, as all good spacemen are, because for every one pound of weight you throw into space, you need 10,000 pounds of fuel.

Even today, the debate rages around the fringes of the space program, as to whether or not it is all worthwhile; could the money be better used on poverty programs, and with the Earth in such a mess, why bother with space anyway?

Every explorer, every inventor, every single person engaged on a quest for the past five thousand years has suffered the same mind-numbing challenge. How to prove that the advancement of knowledge is worth the effort and drama that is always associated with a radical change in our attitude.

But when you come right down to it, it is always a single person who achieves this seemingly Herculean feat - and in the short space of a single day, the newest conquest to challenge your perceptions passes into familiarity, and we start the process all over again. Within the span of another day, chances are you will not even remember what it was that so perturbed you about the "new" information you had to cope with, just hours previously.

Your mind is infinitely expandable, as is your capacity to learn new things. It is your attitude that determines the what, when, how, and why of what you choose to learn, and what you do with it. It is also your attitude that attracts or repels other people. You've heard this before - your outer stance is controlled and dominated by your inner stance - and if you hold some measure of uncomfortableness deep inside the well of your soul, then it can't help but be reflected in your external projection to the outside world.

Just as your body quickly reflects what you eat - eat well, look well, feel well - so does your external stance reflect what you are thinking - look good, feel good, do good.

When someone is attracted to you, while they "see" all the external signs, they "feel" all the inner signs.

And if there is too great a perceived difference between the observation and the feeling, then it is unlikely that they will willingly enter your sphere of influence. Even If you project the very best possible picture imaginable, they will still sniff out the truth - because the ability to feel something that is right comes from within our intellect, and is heightened by our experience and our knowledge.

Instinctively you always know when something is right, just as you instinctively know when something is wrong. It takes a conscious effort to override your feelings, and do the opposite of what you know to be the correct thing. The same is true of your ability to sense when someone is telling you a truth. If it doesn't "feel" right, you have to fight very hard to accept what is being said.

The bottom line, then, is that you will always attract the type of person that you are most in tune with, mentally, and spiritually. The depth of that attraction will depend on many things - just as its longevity will be dependent on many things. Clearly, then, you must become aware of who you really are, and who you really want to be.

This awareness will drive your inner stance, and focus your endeavours into those areas that are the most important to you. And once your inner self is "true", you will attract everyone of a like attitude. The possibilities, potentially, are limitless.

In Australia, there is a phenomena called "mateship", that has been the point of much speculation and research. Initially, it was viewed as a peculiarly male attitude, very much involved with drinking, gambling, swearing, and chasing after women. It's public origins go all the way back to the Boer War, where the first Australian contingent of soldiers, ill-prepared and poorly trained, found themselves in conditions that, at first experience, appeared to be more deadly than the Boers!

"Mateship" was a simple process - to survive, everyone had to help everyone else. And with the great Australian tendency for improvisation, these farmers and clerks soon found that together there was very little they couldn't accomplish.

Today, the informal rules of "mateship" allow you to mix and drink with like-minded people, and never discover their names!

It allows you to offer your help freely, willingly, and cheerfully, no matter the task, and walk away with no more than a casual "thanks mate" in return.

The very essence of "mateship" is that you will do for someone else something you would probably not do for yourself.

And it is the attitude of "mateship" that draws people together, not the rewards, emotionally, or physically.

"Mateship" assumes that you are friendly, interested, willing to share, and just as willing to participate. You can be a "mate" but not necessarily a friend. Alternatively, you can be a "best" friend, yet still be a good "mate". It is very much in the eye of the beholder.

When you get right down to it, there's a lot to be said about "mateship" and its assumed values.

The next time you see someone smiling, and feel yourself irresistibly drawn towards them, remember this.

It is your inner self that is attractive to them, and it is your like-mindedness that will quickly jump the barriers of ignorance, race, colour, creed, or timing.

And when you get right down to it, what's the worst thing that can happen?

# THE CUNNING DUALITY OF FREDRICK FOSDYKE

Even when it seems
that all around you has gone mad,
and nothing will work,
don't lose hope.
As you read about the trials
and tribulations of Fredrick Fosdyke,
observe that all it takes
is an enquiring mind,
and the will-power to see it through,
whatever the odds.
This is what true personal power
is really all about!

Deep in his heart, Harry had always known that his best friend, Fredrick Fosdyke, would one day come to no good. Always drifting off in Transient School, always thinking about something that had absolutely nothing to do with anything worthwhile at all. To the others at the VRA, those classmates who jeered and taunted him relentlessly at the Virtual-Reality Academy, he was a feather-brained jerk, always knowing the difficult answers, sometimes even showing signs of true genius, but never fitting in with their self-styled hedonistic fashion of the day.

Fredrick was that unique human being who's mind was always galloping off in a new direction, always seeking solutions to seemingly unsolvable problems. Never content to leave curiosity alone, Fredrick could always be found where trouble was brewing, his tattered cap askew, his eyes alive with questions.

And now he lay inert, or, thought Harry to himself, taking extra care not touch anything at the death scene, those few bits of Fredrick's body that were still recognisable lay inert, and were definitely finished with life as Harry knew of it, for a long, long, time.

Harry scratched idly at his balding head, hunched up his shoulders in defeat, then waved the waiting medicos over, to lay claim to the bloodied and shattered remains of his once best friend.

"They didn't get his soul, you know," a soft voice whispered in Harry's water-filled ear. He turned slowly like a lumbering bear, fixing his fifty year old cop's eyes on the speaker. A small man, neatly dressed, face in shadow, hands thrust deep into coat pockets, the drizzle forming small rivers of sparkling water where it gathered and was repelled from the small-force field that covered his hat. Nothing in his slightly frumped manner hinted at his intentions, or seemingly postured a menace.

"Why do you say that?" Harry asked, his curiosity overcoming his instincts. Something didn't feel right, it hadn't from the time he had received the emergency call at home. But his gut told him that this dapper little man wasn't any real threat, and his friend Fredrick had spent a lifetime collecting all manner of strange, bizarre friends, of all shapes and sizes, from every level of the six available Strata, and before that, from all over the O/S. This could easily be one of them.

"I saw it all. They didn't get his soul," the stranger stated emphatically. He removed one hand covered in a pale goatskin glove from the depths of his coat pocket, and pointed to a small puddle of slime and mud in which rested a single finger, hooked in the rictus of death like a cracked parrot's beak. Harry scratched his head again, comfortable in the thought that this little man was well qualified to have been one of Fredrick's friends. Obviously weird, and as mad as a hatter. Who bothered to wear simskins in this day and age?

"Did you know him?" Harry asked, his detective's natural caution preventing him from naming the victim. A sudden chill ran down his spine as the little man suddenly looked up into his eyes, the red light from the flashing beacons emphasising the hollows under his cheekbones, making his face look like a well-worn skull. The rain repelling force-field that surrounded his hat flickered with a greenish-blue glow, further creating the illusion that Harry was staring into the face of a ghost.

"Yes, like you, I've known Freddie Fosdyke for years. I still do!" he said, laughing softly as he slunk off into the night, only to be temporarily restrained by a uniformed officer at the floating barrier, then waved on his way at a nod from Harry. He could find him again, easily, or why would the strange little man have slipped him a business card? Harry turned it over in his hand, smoothing the water from its surface, and peered at it in an attempt to read the tightly hand-written flowing script.

`Temporal, Majestic, and Intra-Strata Problems Solved' it said, and Harry suddenly felt the chills start to run up and down his spine again, causing him to hunch his shoulders over, crack-ing his neck cartilages in the process. He held the card up to his face, the better to see the neat lines of small print that scooted across the bottom, so cramped they seemed to almost fall off the edge of the card.

`The difficulty in this plane of existence is that the longer you partake of it, the harder it is to remember the other dimen-sion you have forsaken.

If you believe in the absolute integrity and indestructibil-ity of your soul, then you too can Revert At The Sparking of the C-MOS-FET'

Harry almost tore the card in half, his sudden fury at this seemingly stupid and vacuous mumbo-jumbo boiling to the top of his brain like a volcano. For relative years now, there had been rumours of some out-of-the-way group fostering the intransigent attitude that the techno-migrants were "captives" of some higher intelligence civilisation, spread out amongst the six Strata against their will. Nothing could be further from the truth.

Harry always felt an immense sense of frustration whenever he came across such drivel, but freedom to be stupid in the six Strata was guaranteed by the Individual Rights Chip, and that was that. Every person was free to develop their intellect, and direct the shape of their lives, in any direction they chose. The only limitation was the absolute preservation of the environmental energy balance.

He breathed deeply, quieting his heart, which had suddenly started to bash his ribcage in anger. He slipped the offending card into his pocket, and started to walk back to his car, the last image of his friend Fredrick looming over him like a nightmare. Somehow, seeing just the tattered remains of someone made it seem all the more unreal.

Harry sighed, letting his mind recover from his shock. Why would someone take out such a harmless crank like Fredrick? A timid, curious man, who had never harmed a living soul in his whole life, and as far as Harry knew, not even squashed a pseudoant or electrobug! He shook his head, almost blindly stepping right through a thin and spindly plain-clothes cop who had been looking for him. He frantically grabbed at the apparition, swaying like a drunk.

"Sorry," Harry muttered under his breath, bouncing off the other cop's personal force-field. "Sorry."

" 's okay, Harry. Do ya wanta details?" The Irish-Italian accent fought its way out between wads of synthetic chewing tobacco and bubblegum, but then, Angelito Valmorbida, or just plain Angie to his close associates, was not one known for the finer graces of good grooming. But a better investigative cop you would never find on any of the four hundred PCB's that made up their unique world.

Harry nodded, slouching down somewhat, to match the lower stature of his partner. He flicked the small button-switch on his cuff, allowing his repellant force-field to bloom out and cover them both, keeping the worst of the freezing sleet from slipping down their necks, and aggravating his tired bones.

"Wella, everyting 'hokay until twelve-ten relative Universal time, thena the Local 897th. Precinct registered a Halo Disturbance that ran six and six on da Scare Scale. They got a floater down here within seconds, seen nothing, were about to go home, when da poopa hit the sleet." Harry smiled at his partner's mixed metaphor, mulling over what kind of device could generate enough energy to go six-six on the Halo Disturbance Scale.

"Any idea what it was?" Harry asked, passing a synthmint over to his partner, its edible wrapper already dissolving in the humid air, leaving sticky tracks all over his fingers.

"Na. Something that big could tear a hole between all four hundred boards, and we don't got anything like that anywhere that I know off no more. Outlawed from the start, remember?" Harry nodded his agreement. Ever since it had been discovered that the intensity and frequency of the super cooled gallium arsinide plasma lasers, or SCGAPL's as they were know as, created vicious atmospheric disturbances that threatened the very stability of the Universe, all Field Effect Transmissions had been outlawed, and the devices that produced them destroyed.

The electromagnetic generators that replaced the SCGAP lasers were just as good, if not a little bulkier, but within a generation or two, it was expected that this slower, clumsier, but less individually satisfying form of earth shaping would be totally accepted by the migrants. No one needed to point out that their very existence depended on it.

"Go on," Harry muttered, chewing his synthmint.

"Well, it'sa all ona bubble, ya can see it for yourself." With that, Angie fired up what looked like a miniature hand-held colour computer, with an add-on bubble memory disc. A stunningly sharp image swam into the tiny screen, flicked and rolled for a second, then settled down. Angie took up the commentary as the fast-moving camera angles provided by the life-support monitors zoomed into the scene. "It went like this, see. First a three dimensional hole appears 'bout six meters off the grass, just over there. Then these three hoods appear, wearing repellers and optical disguises. They rush up to the stiff, snatch something offa him, then blast him from three sides. Before the floater can get to them, they're back into the hole, which zips shut, and it's all over but the singing."

Harry scratched at his head again, screwing his face up in the process. "Their personal shields contracted to get them down to board level, that I can see. But how did they get back up?" he asked. Angie just shrugged his shoulders. To him, those sort of details were irrelevant. He wanted to taste the blood of the killers, and just as soon as possible. How they worked their particular type of magic was of little interest to the tough cop, who's simple philosophy on life often turned his superior's hair grey.

Harry smiled, content to pursue his curiosity later. He pushed his hands down further into his long coat, as if to help warm them against the biting chill of the induced storm. His world might well reflect the absolute pinnacle of technology, as known to man, but it still managed to bug the living daylights out of the average citizen!

"So we're looking for someone that has access to a space-worm or better, can locate and home in on a single manbios from inside a nutrino-derived FET shield, and has enough generator power to go six-six on the HDS while they're doing it." Harry stroked his chin, furrowing his brow in concentration. "And they have enough clout topsides to come and go undetected. That about it?" he added.

"Yeah. You make it sound so simple!" Angie replied, slapping his partner on the back. They both started off towards Harry's car, sitting calmly forty centimetres off the pavement, dual red and blue beacons beating at each other as they flashed furiously inside their small force screens. It looked impressive, but was anything but, as any cop knew who had tried to chase down any speeding vehicle in one.

"I'ma sorry about Fredrick," Angie offered, opening the hatch for Harry.

"Thanks, he was on my intake. We went through VRA together. Me, I couldn't understand half of what they were getting at."

"Anda Fredrick could?"

"Yeah, Freddie could. So fast, and so well, he was actually creating images of his own before we graduated. Had this idea that if he could design a truly portable VR Generator, he could solve most of the problems that were anticipated with the boilover. Used to send the Teachers nuts, not to mention the Techo's!"

"Ana did he?" Angie asked, his curiosity peaked. Harry paused, considering the question. Did Fredrick succeed with his wild idea? Harry suddenly realised that he had never bothered to find out, and a sudden flush of embarrassment turned his neck and face puce-pink. He shrugged his shoulders, slipping into the small cockpit of the Patrol Floater.

"Don't know. See you at the office." The clamshell door slid silently down after him as he hit the "Locate" button, waited until the compumap flashed its acceptance of his instruction, selected the icon that represented his home, then sat back into the plastic seat as the floater accelerated, whining out into the central traffic flow. Outside, the sleet and wind went about their preprogrammed jobs of making the conditions thoroughly miserable, quickly filling the wake left by the speeding floater with all manner of refuse. While Minendo was basically a clean environment, there always seemed to be little bits and pieces of things flying around, like motes of dust in the late afternoon sun.

Far from achieving the Designer's ambition of preserving elements of Topside normalcy, all the rubbish did was make Minendo look perpetually grubby!

Harry reached out and touched the vision controls, scanning the news faxes and inbound optical transmissions, anything to keep his mind off the disturbing memory of Fredrick's unfortunate demise. Angie's question still rattled around in his mind, so he decided to honour Freddie's memory, and pursue the issue first thing in the morning. If Freddie had made the breakthrough he was so positive was possible, then he'd find out about it, and put Freddie's ghost to rest.

His beeper suddenly went berserk, and instinctively he snapped the video switch on the small dashboard, punching in his personal code. The small screen that carried the moving map display flicked, blanked, then blossomed into life with the chaotic image of Angie, pointing at an unseen camera.

"They've done it again!" he shouted, ducking the swirling blades of an optiocopter that threatened to cut his head off. "Same MO as before, but this time they took out a Commissioner and two Councillors." Harry studied the digital video images of the new crime scene, again personally revolted at the horrific carnage the mysterious murderers were dispatching so willy nilly. The tiny screen only gave him a small field of vision, but he could clearly see bits of human flesh and limbs lying askance, some floating and bobbing where ever manufacturing imperfections had created indentations in the orange-brown PCB, allowing the spent blood to pool.

"Send the bubble to my home," Harry said tiredly, referring to the bubble memory chip that would hold all the different video angles, and commentary. "I'll still see you in the morning."

" 'hokay, Boss. See ya!" On the screen, Angie turned and started to walk towards the milling crowd, just as his image was replaced with that of Control Central. Captain Bellamy's unsmiling face swam into view, over the top of a flashing screen instruction that said, "Overriding local signal".

"Harry," the Captain barked, as if he were talking to a recently trained pseudodog.

"Captain," Harry barked back. Both men smiled, physically relaxing. They were long-time friends, comfortable with each other's strengths and weaknesses, and outside their very necessary professional relationship, still shared many off-duty hours communicating with each other.

"Well, Harry, here we go again," the older man said quietly, bending forward towards the unseen camera. The effect of this was to create the illusion that he was leaning into the front of the cop car, to sit on Harry's lap.

"Yes, looks like it. How much do you know?" Harry asked, sinking back into his seat, letting the cop car carry on getting him home automatically.

"Not much. Just the side-band of your last message, and the videocomps of Fosdyke's murder. Sorry, he was a good friend of yours, wasn't he?"

"Yeah." Harry thought for a second, scratching at his head, a habit he seemed to have suddenly adopted for the duration of this particular investigation. "Did you check the EMS levels?" he finally asked. The total energy available, both human and otherwise, was constantly monitored by a series of Electromagnetic Management Systems spread out across the six Strata, just like in the old days where electrical energy consumption was measured and delivered for a price by Power Companies.

The big difference this time, was that if the EMS didn't do their job exactly, perfectly, and before-time, the six Strata could well fold in on themselves, annihilating Minendo, and every presence in it.

"First thing we did. Whatever they're doing, their power source comes from outside. The manbios are down by the equivalent factor of an additional three presences, and we're showing a small leak between boards three and four. Probably caused by the field-effect-transmissions when they broke through with the space-worm."

"Yeah, that makes sense. Have you got ID's on the deceased?" Harry asked, a nagging thought starting somewhere in the murky recesses of his tired mind.

"Yes, exactly as called by Angie Valmorbida. The crime-comp is searching for possible links between the four people removed, and is also searching the entire migrant data bases to establish individual locations at the time of both incidents." Harry thought about that for a minute, while his floater zigged and zagged around the CapaCityTowers complex, seeking his humble home buried deep within its bowels. A modest man of modest means, even in this, the most high-tech city ever built on Earth or any other Planet, he preferred the peace and quiet of the outer fringes of the board, rather than the more ritzy central core.

Besides, from time immortal, cops lived quiet, reserved lives, far away from the flash and dash of their counterparts, the criminal element that always seemed to balance the best intentions of any society. He smiled to himself at the sudden thought that even in the strangest of circumstances, Mother Nature, or perhaps God? always managed to balance things up!

"Okay, enough. I'm practically brain dead. Let's take this up again in the morning," Harry said, fighting back a huge yawn. The Captain grunted, snapping the connection before Harry could wish him "good night", but that's the way he was. To most people, blunt to the point of eruptive rudeness. To those that worked with him, tightly focussed with no time for fools, but a man who delivered on his promises, and could be trusted, utterly. Two qualities that were in short supply in the New Age of disaster.

Harry's floater glided to a silent stop under the dripping eves of his apartment, and the door hissed open to let him out. He was so tired he barely managed to switch the car off as he struggled out, wrestling with his damp coat.

The next thing he was conscious of was the holographic window pouring buckets of artificial sunlight into his face, and his egg timer shrieking at him to attend the breakfast table. He took the time to quickly scan the pile of faxes his video had spewed out onto the floor while he had slept the sleep of the dead, occasionally mumbling to himself as a specific fact or detail registered, juggling the flimsy faxes between slivers of burnt toast dripping with undercooked raw egg.

"Harry, I have a call for you," a pleasant female voice called from the corner of the untidy room. Harry waved one hand carelessly, almost sending globs of yellow egg yoke slithering onto the electrostatic field that fought tirelessly to keep the floor clear. It briefly sparked in pseudo anger, as if to remind him to watch his manners.

"Accepted", he mumbled, not bothering to look at the screen, acknowledging the voice of the auto-summoner.

"Hi, Harry. It's Mike. Angie asked me to run down some reports and things for you, how do you want them?" Harry stopped in his tracks, a sliver of toast poised at his gaping mouth. He wondered what Angie was up to now.

"Downlink them to my car," he muttered, catching a drool of yellow egg just before it broke away from the bottom side of the toast.

"Okay, Harry. No sweat. See ya!" the young datavoice said to an empty room.

As Harry emerged from the microwave cleaner he wondered briefly what it was that had worried him so much last night, but his mind had dispatched the information to the nether regions, deep within his subconscious somewhere, so he let it go and headed out into an artificially brilliant sun-lit morning. He knew better than to try and force something out, before it was ready.

With his floater safely programmed to take him to his office, he tapped his wrist controller and focussed on the small video screen that faced him.

"Speak to me," he commanded jokingly, happy with the thought that he at least had the energy to crack a funny, even if it was only with a dumb machine!

"Okay Harry, nice to talk to you again," the datavoice called `Mike' said. "Now, first up Angie asked me to track down the last stored movements of one Fredrick Fosdyke, since confirmed as extinct in this Strata......." Harry winced at the emotionless, rational description the master computer had allocated to his friend's sudden death, sucking his breath in between clenched teeth as he paused the data flow. As his pulse lowered, he released the image, which continued on in the same measured tone, as if it hadn't been disturbed in the slightest, ".....since twelve fourteen relative Universal Time, 2002. Do you want the data by day, in reverse order, or ..."Harry cut the computer off, suddenly remembering what had bothered him the night before.

"Quit current data. Specific retrieve," he ordered, watching as the video image of the talking head warped and twisted as it tried to keep up with the sudden change in programme Harry was demanding.

"Subject?" it snapped back, its voice several octaves higher, imitating an angry clerk in the Public Service of long ago. Even in Minendo, City Hall still ran things, as its computers enjoyed reminding everyone at every opportunity!

"Fosdyke, Fredrick, migrant intake twenty-oh-six-six-niner foxtrot. Specific data on miniature Virtual Reality project, all Strata, Topsides, O/S, and all time frames, in ascending chronological order."The screen rippled with fuzzy colours as the video circuit tried to imagine what image Harry would like the data presented by, then simply gave up, switching to a plain white background with a set of ruby red lips in the centre.

City Hall has never had a sense of humour!

"Time zone 1995, month seven, Virtual Reality Academy number #343, USA, subject submitted Patent designs for a portable Virtual Reality unit with an assessed reality performance of 89.90675%. Patent refused. Subject applied for second assessment in month eleven, same year, same VRA, reality performance now 93.76504%. Patent refused. Relative Time zone 1997, month three, Strata five, Virtual Reality Minendo, subject created Halo Disturbance level seven-four, damage sustained on PCB #45473, casualties one hundred and fifty nine manbios units. This event, in conjunction with others of that time frame, led to the banning of all SCGAPL devices in month five. Time zone 1998, month ten, VRA #343 USA, subject applies for third assessment of earlier device, reality performance now 99.8996%. Patent finally refused after full-board review, in perpetuity, month twelve. Subject data-stream ends. No further data on this specific request relative to subject available from any source."

Harry suddenly sat up in his seat, bumping his head on the plasto roof lining as he did so. "Did you say that he applied for a third Patent at the VRA?" he asked. The lips seemed to quiver, as if being asked to repeat something, was more than they could bear.

"Yes." The lips blurred and started to thin out in the corners in anticipation of Harry's next question, which wasn't long in coming. Machines were still quicker than their almost human counterparts.

"He actually applied at the VRA in 1998?" he asked incredulously.

"Yes." As far as the lips were concerned, a fact was a fact, and the video sensor found it hard to cope with the rising body temperature of its user, uncertain as to what images it should create to placate him. It decided, logically, that the lips would do, but rapidly changed both the colour and the shape, not wanting to be discarded as a communication failure, or wilful program.

What it had not sensed was that Harry was deep in thought, completely ignoring the video and the data link, and completely immune to the antics of the datavoice. He now had two bits of incredible information to work with, and his cop's instincts were fairly buzzing.

The floater pulled into the Precinct Station, and Harry, whistling a tuneless melody between stained teeth, eased himself out and walked briskly into his office, ignoring the repetitive calls of the baffled datavoice.

He punched his desk monitor on, ignored his electronic mail, and went straight to his personal, double coded and locked data files. A few short key strokes later and he was sitting back in his chair, feet on the desk, listening to his PC summarise the personal and professional histories of the Commissioner and the two Councillors who had been killed the night before. It didn't take long to find what he wanted.

"Repeat last ten seconds," he ordered. The same sulky voice that had spoken to him in his floater, rearranged its priorities, and complied with his request.

"Time zone 1994 to 1998, subject Ronald Kent served as Chief-of-Staff VRA #343 USA. Migrated under instructions from the Director-General, relative time zone 1999, month one. Confirmed Commissioner, Strata five, on arrival." Bingo! Suddenly he had three pieces of the puzzle.

Harry closed his eyes, letting his cop's suspicious mind roam free around his hunches, his guesses, and his instinct, certain that he was headed in the right direction. The age old triad of Motive, Means, and Opportunity were still the best place to anchor an investigation, even in the most sophisticated environment man had ever created.

He was sure he now had a Motive. The Means would have to be investigated Topside and O/S, and he was sure that the Opportunity would become more apparent when he managed to nail down the Means. He looked at the computer's screen, his blurred reflected image staring back at him.

"Interrupt. Direct classified call to Oscar-Sierra, contact niner-niner-six, connect now," he ordered. The video rippled its discontent at having to change its mind, yet again, but within seconds, Captain Bellamy's rugged face swam into view, just as a protective scrambler force-field erupted around Harry and his desk. From outside, it looked like he had been suddenly attacked by a dense, impenetrable dirty grey fog, that flickered at the edges with an angry electric spark.

"You've put some of the pieces together," the Captain barked, leaning forward so far in his chair that it looked to Harry as if he was about to fall out of the screen and into his lap.

"Yes. But I need your boys to tie some things down for me."

"What kind of things?"

"Research all contacts between Fosdyke and Ronald Kent. Find out who, when, and why Kent was allocated migration. And I need an HD map for the last five years."

"For Minendo?"

"Yes."

"Standard or relative?"

"Standard. But you asked that first question as if there is somewhere else as well. Have you created another Virtual Reality Environment?"

"Maybe, maybe not. I'll get back to you," the Captain snapped, disconnecting before Harry could pursue the point. But his agile mind fairly romped with enthusiasm at this new thought, because if there was a new destination for the migrants, a sister destination to Minendo, then he might have just been given a small piece of information that would help solve another side of the triad. Means.

He punched up Angie's communication code, and waited for an acknowledgement.

"Hi ya bossman, what'sa up?" the effervescent young Cop asked, unfazed at being rudely woken up from a deep, and apparently much needed sleep.

"Need you."

"'hokay. On my way." Harry sat back, using his wrist controller to reorientate the video back to where he had interrupted it, before he had spoken to the far away Captain Bellamy.

"Continue with data," he said, leaning back into his chair, and dismissing the security fog all in one fluid motion. With a loud crack, the electrostatic security barrier disappeared, leaving the smell of ozone in the air, as if a thunderstorm had just passed through.

"What subject?" the sulky voice asked, this time from the face of a well-presented middle aged woman, similar to the newscasters of old. The datavoice had tired of the lips, and was equally tired trying to anticipate Harry's rapid mood swings.

"Councillors, recently deceased. Addendum to Kent data". The screen flickered almost imperceptibly, and the face smiled.

"Continuing report. Time zone 1994, month two, VRA #343 USA, Professor Jon Johannesen appointed to Physical Research Laboratory, with Doctor Edward Summerville appointed his assistant. Both men awarded migration status time zone 1999, month four, appointed Councillors of Strata-Three and Strata-One respectively on arrival."

"So we're looking for the person that awards migration status Topside and O/S, and the person who appoints TOA's in here," Harry muttered to himself.

"I beg your pardon?" the video asked somewhat haughtily, annoyed at the molecular level by the seemingly irrelevant data.

"None of your business," snapped Harry, spotting Angie as he entered the Squad room.

"Hi ya Harry, what's up?" Angie asked, a cheeky grin splitting his handsome face from ear to ear.

"I need you to do some leg work," Harry answered, pointing to the other side of his desk. Angie quickly sat down.

"First, I need to track the physical movements and habits of Fredrick Fosdyke. Any one month period will do, but it has to be thorough."

"Okay."

"And I also need to know who is responsible for the appointment of Strata Officials." Angie's brow furrowed in sudden concentration.

"But Harry, migrants come here with a designated job and title, don't they?" he asked.

"That's what I thought, too. And I guess in most cases, it's true. But sniff around the central core and see what you can find." Angie shrugged his shoulders, it wasn't for him to reason why, and, besides, in the three short relative years he had been assigned to Harry as his assistant, he had learned more about being a good cop than in the previous fifteen years he had spent on the crime infested streets of New York.

Harry watched his young partner leave, then reached into his coat pocket and pulled out the wrinkled business card he had been given the night before. He dialled the communication code and watched, fascinated, by the custom designed screen that popped onto his video. Swirls, 3D geodetic shapes, and a myriad of colours flowed over each other as the little man's face swam into focus. He was obviously a programmer, or knew a very good one, Harry thought to himself.

"I've been waiting for your call," the dapper man said, with the same insane chuckle rattling around his throat as he had made at the death scene. Harry smiled back, now completely sure that he was on firm ground. Confidence was often the precursor of genuine knowledge, and he suddenly looked forward to the conversation. He activated the security fog again, waited until he was sure it had settled all around, then sat back in his chair and put his feet up on the desk top.

"You have a means, or are in direct contact with, someone from Topsides, from Oscar-Sierra," he said, watching for the telltale eye movements that would precede an evasive answer. The video screen had sensors at both ends which monitored heart rate, body temperature, and brain-wave patterns, so lying was almost impossible. But there were always shades of the truth, and Harry believed that his gut was still the best monitor of what was really going down, his natural distrust of machines surfacing again. The little man just smiled, almost serenely, Harry thought. But his eyes were firmly fixed on Harry's, and didn't so much as flinch as he answered.

"Yes. Just like you."

"I see. Is it an official link?" Harry asked.

"None of your business."

"I can make it so," Harry said, the lack of threat in his voice if anything giving an even harder edge to his statement. The little man still didn't waver. Either he was used to pressure from the cops, or he thought his contacts had the clout to keep them in their place. Harry didn't like this thought, snapping out of his introspective thoughts as the man replied.

"Why bother? I'll answer any question you care to ask, there's no need for you to interfere in my little enterprise." Harry considered his options, finally deciding on the middle course of apparent reasonableness. He could always change his mind later, and besides, his gut still told him that the dapper man was no recognisable threat.

"Okay. First question. Why the scam and mumbo jumbo about other dimensions, and this nonsense about `Reverting At The Sparking of the C-MOS-FET'?" he asked.

"What better cover for someone that has access to the O/S?" the little man counted. "Besides," he added, shifting in his seat so that his face seemed to loom over Harry, "I've turned my ability into a thriving business. I provide a datastream both ways, and just like the Mediums of olden days, I provide a channel, an out-let as it were, for people's anxieties."

"Do you do Seances? Appearances? All that stuff?"

"No. Much better than that. I actually get derived digital video and play it to the customer first hand. They provide the questions, and my O/S contacts find the live personalities - if they are still usable, that is, and generate the computer graphics necessary to provide accurate images and answers."

"Howcome you've never been detected?" Harry asked, more as a means of giving his mind time to digest what he was hearing than of trying to find something out. He was both amused at the ingenuity of the little man, and horrified at the implications. Trouble was, he wasn't too sure which emotion was the strongest.

"I don't consume any energy that's monitored here in Minendo," the dapper man replied. Harry was stunned. Maybe, just maybe, the big "M", Means, was about to come rumbling through his videocomm, from the mouth of a modern-day shyster.

"What? That's impossible. Everything, both O/S, and here in Minendo, is monitored in both actual and relative time-streams to the quadrillionth of an erg."

"No it's not. There are secret read-only-memory, bio-in-tergrated-intelligent-operating-systems, you know them as ROMBIOS, that go all the way back to the original program-mers. I'm not going to tell you where they are, because you could shut them down, and put us all out of business. But the inherent programming subset allows those in the know to tap into a nutrino stream that has more transmission power than anyone knows what to do with. And the fact that I do what I do, and you have never suspected it previously, proves that it works, doesn't it?" Harry reluctantly nodded his agreement. It did at that, and this funny little man was right. If he could find the subsets, he would shut the illegal power stream down if he could. Time to change subjects.

"How long have you known that Fredrick wasn't really in here?" he asked, hoping to catch the little man off guard.

"Since he first arrived. It was my communication system with the O/S that drew him to me in the first place." Harry nodded to himself, it was all starting to stack up.

"Why?"

"He needed to tap into the ROMBIOS source to maintain his presence, just in case the O/S suffered a power spike that threw the grid over to an alternative generator."

"Explain that to me," Harry asked, baffled. He was a cop, not a computer freak, and while he was more than grateful for what computer science had done for him, he never pretended to totally understand what it was all about. The little man smiled, enjoying the prospect of tickling Harry's curiosity. Sometimes a little knowledge went a long way!

"Well, if the O/S grid switched, even for a millionth of a second, there'd be a phase shift in all the computer generated images. Not much, granted, but enough for someone like yourself, or a technician, to notice if you were watching for it." Harry sighed, waving his hand around in frustration.

"Could you put that in plain language?" he pleaded. The little man smiled again.

"If you were directly interfacing with me, say, on the street where we met last night, and the power cycled as I described, I would appear to blink out from your perspective." Harry sighed again, deeply, deciding to let this particular issue go, not sure if pursuing it was worth the brain agony of trying to understand.

"Are there others using these RAMBIOS for illegal power generation?" he asked, trying a different tack. The little man hesitated, as if he were turning the question over and over in his mind.

"Not yet. At least, I don't think so. But you never can tell." His image faded from the video, and inspite of Harry punching back the little man's code, the screen stayed blank. Which meant he had dedicated control over his communicator, as well as his own free unlimited power source! Something he'd have to chase down another time, he thought to himself, ruefully.

He stood up, killed the security fog, and stretched his arms up over his head to get the kinks out of his shoulders and neck. It seemed the older he got, the earlier his aches and pains started every day.

What a case!

Unknown assassins with a space-worm, secret power sources so powerful that they provided unlimited two way access with the O/S, and little dapper men who earned a living out of conjuring up ghosts of long dead relatives out of computer data files and CGI.

Incredible though it seemed, Harry was forced into believing the evidence as each complex piece turned from hunch and guess, to hard, verifiable fact. Trouble was, he didn't know exactly what he could do about it here in Minendo. He was just about to expand on this thought and sit back down at his desk when suddenly everything around him went grey, wavered and flickered rapidly, then disappeared like so much used security fog.

Harry instinctively snapped on his cuff controller, throwing his force-field out to about ten centimetres all around his body, and watched as he suddenly seemed to be standing on a small shiny disc, floating in a perpetual sea of dirty orange mist. Overhead, a radiant blue and orange light flickered, sending bolts of razor sharp white light down past his face. His disc attached itself to one of the bolts, and suddenly he started to rise as if he were in an elevator.

Which I am, he thought to himself, knowing that the proton stream he was travelling in was surrounded by a carbonfibre optic casing. At the speed of light, and even at Harry's relative slower elapsed timeframe, it only took micro-seconds for the plasma disc to reach its destination. Harry recognised the synoptic terminal for what it was, nothing more than a super high-tech bus stop, and stepped off the plasma disc. Suspended in nothingness, he waited patiently, his hands stuffed into his crumpled coat.

The first time he had done this he had been so scared he could not willingly open his eyes!

Within a few heartbeats, a room folded itself around him, and Captain Bellamy, a woman, and two unknown men dissolved into focus, their bodies arriving just a fraction of a second before the floor and the furniture, creating the illusion that they were disjointedly flying through space. Within another heartbeat, Virtual Reality reigned supreme, and Harry took the liberty to sit down first in a form-fitting chair that had been thoughtfully provided for him.

"Harry, these two gentlemen represent the President, and Marion you've met before," Captain Bellamy said, pointing towards the svelte blond woman with lean, Slavic features, and penetrating blue eyes. Harry nodded to the two Presidential Aides, feasting his eyes on Marion Harper, the VRA Psychologist who had been his last touch of human flesh.

"Hello Marion," he said, his mind struggling to remember the perfumes and textures of her tanned body.

"Hello Harry, you look good," she said. Harry laughed, embarrassed.

"I can look however they choose," he replied, inwardly pleased that she was comfortable with being personal with a completely computer generated three dimensional holographic image. The Captain drew their eyes with a deliberate cough, waiting until he had their full attention.

"Okay Harry, you can socialise later. You wanted an HD map of the last five years, Fosdyke's relationship with Kent, and the details on Kent's migration. Correct?"

Harry nodded. The tone in the Captain's voice told him all he needed to know about the Presidential Aides, and he could guess why Marion Harper had become involved. The Captain snapped another holovision into being, and a three dimensional cube filled the space between Harry and his inquisitors. Red and green lines interlaced between a green plane and six mustard-brown coloured rectangles, with little sparking blue and white flashes zipping between all seven strata.

"The green lines are our controlled inputs, the red ones are random. No one had thought to look at the HD's like this, it's revealing, isn't it?" Harry nodded, fascinated with the sheer amount of random, and therefore illegal, activity the model of his world, Minendo, was displaying. Activity that could only mean one thing.

"How many contacts were there?" he asked.

"Wrong question. I'll let the expert fill you in," the Captain snapped, pointing to one of the anonymous Presidential Aides.

"Urh, Sir, while each line represents a transmission, the model is too simplistic to give a qualitative picture. The other consideration is the time duration of each contact." Harry looked at the fresh young face of the adviser as he spoke, wondering if he was using drugs to inhibit body-decomp, or if he really were as young and as innocent as he looked and sounded.

"I'm not sure if I follow you," Harry said, looking at the holovision closely. Using a laser pointer, the adviser singled out a single green line within the cube, which seemed to pulse slowly with a life of its own.

"Look here. This data line is sequenced over a long period, say, around three to four months." He moved the electron-thin light, and selected another green line. "This one is pulsing much faster, indicating a short time frame, say, around fifteen relative minutes." Harry nodded, suddenly understanding the key to the images in the cube. He pointed with his own finger, causing a red line to bend around its shape, like a projected image onto a curved surface.

"So this illegal transmission is about two relative hours long?" he asked.

"Yes."

"Can you tell what was transmitted in either direction?"

"Yes, Sir."

"Have you done a scan and comparison?"

"Of course, Sir. The data is waiting for you to draw it down. But I can save you a lot of time if you wish." Harry stared at the young adviser, suspicious of his overt politeness. He was a computer image, no more substantive than any other manbios centred presence, locked into the VR world of Minendo. The youngster was still a real, live, human being, albeit not for much longer. Perhaps the O/S was in more trouble than he realised.

"Please do," he asked softly, settling back into his chair, wishing he had his office desk to put his feet up on.

"Well, Sir, taking the five standard year period you requested, there are a total of seven hundred random transmissions, ranging from milliseconds to months in standard length. Loosely grouped, they fall into three distinct categories." The Aid tuned his pointer by twisting a small knob, and it suddenly branched out into three different lines of coloured light, each of which attached itself to a different red line running between the green plane and the six mustard-brown coloured rectangles, that represented the six strata of Minendo.

"The first category we've logged runs up to one standard minute, and carries burst transmissions, compiled data, and compressed video. We believe that the original programmers designed this mode to provide feedback to the master controller, allowing for constant monitoring and tuning of the environment you experience within Minendo."

Harry nodded his agreement. He wasn't a computer expert by any means, but being a graduate of the VRA, and having lived in a Virtual Reality Environment for over three relative years, he understood much of what it took to keep Minendo running smoothly. Or at the very least, the appearance of doing so.

"And the second category?" he asked.

"Runs from one to fifteen standard minutes. Definitely illegal, high enough power levels to facilitate real-time transmissions, both data, CGI, and video."

"These are the streams your strange friend uses for his mystic activities," the Captain added. The adviser paused until he was certain that he wouldn't be interrupted again, then continued.

"It's this third stream that the President is really interested in - the one that is obviously being used to sustain artificial VR Personalities in Minendo. It runs anywhere from one standard week all the way to one standard month." Harry shrugged, he had already grown used to the idea that his friend, Fredrick Fosdyke, had used this system, or one like it, for some relative years, and once he had overcome the natural shock of this incredible technological slight-of-mind feat, the broader details were much easier to swallow. And in a very strange way, less threatening.

He nodded silently to himself. Amazing how just the simple process of learning about something reduced the natural fear one tended to experience! And now he had a new piece of information, a very valuable one. The President of the remaining United States was personally interested in this case. And that could only mean one thing.

"How long has the President to live before migration?" he asked softly, watching the eyes of the two "Aides" for any reaction. It wasn't long coming. As if linked by a data-stream sixty-four bit fibre optic cable, two pairs of eyes narrowed in unison, the pupils dilating to half their normal size. Almost at the same split second, they relaxed, outwardly calm and collected, as the brain behind each decided, almost in unison, on the lie that would be told. Harry saved them the trouble.

"Forget it. Captain," he said, turning slightly in his chair, "I thought that once a migration decision was taken, it was irrevocable?"

"It is. Or, at least, it used to be. As you know from first hand experience, once your "personality" and your "life data" are lifted, and you enter the VRA, your material carcass is disposed of. Permanently." Harry still shuddered at the thought, even six standard years after the fact. Somewhere at the back of his mind an idea started to form, but not fast enough for him to grasp it immediately.

So he played his usual trick with his subconscious, and let it suck in the data, all the better to process it, in its own good time.

"Are the conditions in real-time still coming apart at the same rate as they were the last time we spoke?" he asked. The two Aides instantly went into their snake-eye routine again, giving Harry his answer. He decided to try another tack. "Okay, then tell me about the other VR Environment that has spooked you so much."

Marion Harper suddenly jumped into the conversation, taking everyone but Harry by surprise. "Captain, we're getting nowhere fast with all this hooded secrecy. I thought you trusted Harry." The three men and Harry's image turned to look directly at her, as if she had committed a major indiscretion. Harry broke the tension with a small laugh, waving his hands depreciatingly.

"Hell, guys, you don't have to worry about me. I've made the transition. I've been in there now for six standard years, and as far as I can tell, my psyche is coping quite well. And after all," he added softly, almost wistfully, "it's not as if I can actually harm you, is it?"

"That's not the point," Captain Bellamy said, so quietly Harry had to tilt his head slightly to hear him.

"Then what is?" Harry asked, his cop's instincts suddenly on full alert. Captain Bellamy looked at each of the Presidential Aides in turn, then at Marion Harper. Seeing neither approval nor disapproval, he took it upon himself to make the final decision. If he were wrong in his assessment of Harry, then mankind as he knew it was doomed.

"Harry, what it comes down to, is that your friend Fredrick Fosdyke has unleashed the biggest can of worms you could ever imagine."

"By creating his own VR Image in Minendo, while keeping his Corporeal form out here in O/S?" Harry asked.

"Yes. In a nutshell, that's it."

"With a slight twist," added Marion Harper. Harry raised his eyebrows, trying to deduce what could possibly be causing so much concern. Then the idea at the back of his mind suddenly formed completely, and he had it.

Once again, his instinct to let his subconscious mind do its own thing, in its own good time, had paid off.

"You can't find Fosdyke," he offered. All four humans stared at him, amazed at the speed of his accurate guess. This was a problem they had been trying to come to grips with for over ninety six standard hours, yet Harry, a mere shadow of his former self, had arrived at the core issue in just relative minutes. And from far less data than they had to work with.

"Right again. You certainly haven't lost your touch," Marion offered. Harry laughed, looking at his CGI hands.

"Why should I? From my perspective, the only thing that's changed is I now live in Minendo, not New York. Crime rate's a helleva lot lower, people are nicer, and there's no pollution or disease to contend with, other than the crap the programmers left lying around for realism."

"Fine, fine, but let's get back to why we're all here," Captain Bellamy said, his acidic tone cutting across the conversation like a scythe. "We've lost Fosdyke. That is, if we ever had him in the first place. And there's hard evidence that he isn't the only one who's bucked the system, and is doing double-time."

"Are you saying that his presence at the Virtual Reality Academy was as VR Image?" Harry asked, in a way that only a cop can.

"Yes. At least, for part of the time. As far as we can tell, Fosdyke passed PhyPro - the physical processing we all have to go through to qualify - in corporeal form. Then between that process and the integration procedure, he apparently substituted a VR Image so good it remained undetected until your relative yesterday, when he supposedly died in a blaze of molecular glory."

"And he did it in real time, in at least two planes, simultaneously," added Marion Harper.

"How do you know when he made the substitution?"

"We back-checked the manbios levels at the VRA Health Centre where you made your transition. The records show the EMS levels have been consistently one manbios short since that time."

"You got onto this when you checked the EMS levels after his death?"

"Yes. We had no reason to check the original base information, until we turned up three units missing for supposedly four CGI's terminated. That's what started the alarm bells ringing."

"And the others you suspect of doing the same?" The room suddenly went very quiet again, as if the four humans were reconsidering the Captain's decision to tell Harry everything.

"Harry, six months after we activated Minendo, we fired up an identical VR Environment as a control. Same number of migrants, same social structure, same methods of selection, same VRA preparation. But with a few additions based on what we had learned from getting Minendo up, mainly to do with the time-frame rate, and the reality-scope resolution."

"And when the poop hit the fan in Minendo, you checked this parallel VR world and found that something similar had occurred?"

"Yes. Only this time we found that we've been missing three units since their original transition."

"No prizes for guessing that they were the Commissioner and the two Councillors."

"Right again."

"And you can't locate any of these people in real time?"

"No. Not even the faintest glimmer of a clue. For all intents and purposes, they have literally disappeared off the face of the Earth, or what's left of it."

"But how can that be? I thought every living soul now had an identifiable radiation signature?" Harry asked, confused at this turn of events. In his last days in the real world, it had been this atomic signature that had provided the clues the scientists needed to understand how to transition a personality into a computer chip, without destroying its sanity.

"They have. But the satellites, for whatever reason, cannot detect these four missing people." Harry mentally withdrew into himself for a minute, letting the information stroll unfettered around in his mind. He had the same feeling he always experienced when he was close to solving a tough case, but this time the problem seemed so vast, he didn't know where to start pinning it all down.

Using another old-dog trick, he let his emotions settle, and tried to break the problem down into its component parts. Trusting his cop's instincts, he thrust his hands deeper into his coat pockets, and stared at the foursome from under his projected heavily-bushed eyebrows.

"Okay, first things first. Real-time living is still on a predicted count-down to disaster?" he asked no one in particular.

"Yes," replied Marion Harper, "out latest scans show that the Earth's surface temperature will reach one hundred ninety degrees Celsius in five and a half standard years. We're losing population to advanced radiation induced biogenetically-mutated diseases at the rate of three hundred and fifty thousand every standard month, and the suicide rate has escalated far beyond predictions."

"How far?"

"Double the rate at present. Around sixty thousand, world-wide, everyday. And I think that'll just get even worse as time goes on."

"The ordinary people in the street see no solution?"

"Unfortunately, yes. Even with the excellent results from the two VR Environments, we can't move fast enough to reassure everyone that they will have a place in the future."

"Have any of the Isohabitats that were planned got off the ground yet?"

"Yes. Three. One in Alaska, which is now almost totally submerged, one in the Pryenees, and one in Osaka."

"Are they working out?"

"No. As predicted, man does not easily live in a confined, subterranean environment, for long lengths of time. The only real success to date has been with the two VR Environments, Minendo and Duoendo.

"Anything in Space?" The two Presidential Aides did their joint eye-narrowing trick, telling Harry everything he wanted to know without moving their mouths, so he rapidly moved on.

"Then what, exactly, is the danger the three, sorry, four, missing men pose to the VR Project?" he asked. For the third time the room fell absolutely silent, and it was left up to the crusty Captain Bellamy to answer.

"We don't know for sure, but from what has happened in just the last four days - two relative days for you - it appears that they can change a perceived VR, they can enter and leave a VR at will, and they can actually destroy a manbios within a VR any time they choose." Harry's synthetic blood ran cold, suddenly realising the enormous power his friend Fredrick Fosdyke had unleashed on an unsuspecting, and rapidly dying, Earth.

And right at a time when it didn't need anything but a total focus on the problem at hand.

"Then we have to find them," Harry stated in an emotion-less voice.

"And neutralise them," instructed one of the Aides.

"And quickly," added the other, inadvertently answer-ing Harry's earlier question about when the President was scheduled for migration. In view of the not so subtle pressure being applied by the Aides, it must be soon. And Presidents were made to command and lead, not cower in an artificially computer-generated bunker in fear of their very artificial existence being snuffed out by a rogue, supposedly dead, eccentric inventor.

"Has the VR technology advanced sufficiently to allow me direct access to the O/S?" Marion Harper grinned a little smile, self-consciously looking down at her hands. Hopefully, Harry thought to himself, thinking about the last time he had been with her in the flesh just three short standard years ago.

"Yes and no. At least, to the untrained eye, someone that doesn't know what to look for, you could pass for a live human in most static controlled environments." Harry thought about that for a second, then a slow smile started to form, the tips of his lips curling up in a not unattractive way.

"Angie Valmorbida's report stated, and I saw it for myself on the crimepic, that just before Fredrick Fosdyke was so violently eradicated, the killers took a small object out of his hand. I've got three questions." Harry paused, waiting for one of the four humans to take up his challenge. After a quick look around the other three, Captain Bellamy signalled for him to continue.

"Okay, first question. If Fredrick was a computer generated image, like me, but still in control of his body, although I confess I don't really understand that part of it yet, why did the killers have to kill him in Minendo? Why kill him at all? And how do you physically take something from a CGI in a VR Environment like Minendo from the Out Side?" The two Presidential Aides physically moved away from Harry, sinking into their chairs, trying to distance themselves from his incredible questions, the answers to which they obviously didn't have, and equally obviously, scared them half to death. In complete contrast, both Captain Bellamy and Marion Harper positively beamed, and if anything, leaned slightly forward, as if to get closer to Harry's almost perfect three-dimensional holistic self.

"Harry, you've just earned your stripes on this case. I'll let Marion fill you in on the details." Captain Bellamy sat back in his seat, beaming from ear to ear with pride. He had picked Harry originally out of thousands of applicants, more on intuition in the end, so close were the short-listed candidates put up to be the first members of the VR Police Force. And he had been right. Not only did Harry have the ability to dramatically adjust his perspective to the circumstances, he hadn't lost any of his talent in the process.

Marion Harper snapped her own holovision unit on, and three representative temporal worlds appeared, each a different colour. Harry immediately noticed that one world was larger than the other, and had a tiny satellite orbiting it. He correctly guessed that this model represented the Earth. Marion Harper pointed to it with a laser pencil.

"Harry, as you already know, the whole purpose of Minendo was to create a Virtual Reality Environment where the surviving population of the earth could be sent, to live out their "natural" lives in relative peace and harmony."

"We also hoped that it would give us a future beyond the life expectancy of the migrants," Captain Bellamy added.

"Exactly. Because of the incredibly short time frame we're left with, our first choice of a Space Colony has been ruled out, although the Russians and the Chinese are still pushing ahead with something in this area." Marion Harper paused, as if considering what to say next. She moved the pointer to illuminate the blue-grey sphere, looking deep into Harry's synthetic eyes. "At first, we thought a VR Environment in itself could be self-supportive, given an indefinite power supply, and a indestructible shell to house the computers and the Strata required."

"If I remember correctly, one of the ideas at the time of my migration was to combine a deep-space probe with a VRE shell, wasn't it?" Harry asked.

"Yes. But now that we know that the radiation levels are far too high for survival, and that the Earth will cool down again somewhere between one hundred and fifty and two hundred standard years, it seems a better option to keep the VRE's here, safely buried somewhere under ground, like Mount Kosciusko. By a fluke of nature, there's enough blue granite to act as a heat-sink and radiation shield, and all our best predictions show that this area will survive with the minimum earth-form damage." Harry nodded slowly to himself, noting that very little had changed on the O/S since his migration. Still preoccupied with survival, still relying on predictions by "experts", and still trying to reshape the forces of nature to do man's bidding, irrespective of the cost.

"Okay then, let's get back to the point. Unless you've changed the ballgame, there were four inviolate rules that governed the creating and running of a VR Environment."

"A Virtual Reality is only as valid as a unit within it observes it to be. All units in a Virtual Reality must have the same quantum charge. Any interface between a Corporeal unit and a Virtual Reality unit must be conducted in a Virtual Reality Environment. The mind-set of a VR unit must be protected at all costs, even at the expense of a Corporeal unit."

"Exactly. So back to my question. Why kill Fosdyke in Minendo? Surely all they had to do was turn his VR Generator off? Or find his programme link, and spike it? If you stop to think about it, there are literally hundreds of ways you can take out a CGI personality, so why all the drama?" Marion Harper smiled at Harry's forceful questioning, a sad look dimming her eyes.

"Look at these spheres. Think of them as the Earth, Minendo, and Duoendo. Imagine that the generators and the power source are here," she said, pointing to the Earth, "and that the VRE's multiplex commdata streams flow like this." With a snap of her wrist controller, thousands of tiny coloured lines started to flow to and from the three spheres, but always only to one sphere from the earth's position, creating an inverted "V" shape."

"You're deliberately limiting a migrant's ability to experience a VR to just the one designated Environment?" Harry asked.

"Yes. We are. But your friend Fosdyke's VR Generator jumps that limitation. Look." The lines representing the two way data streams between earth and the two VR Environments suddenly became jumbled, like so much spaghetti, the three spheres almost completely hidden by the mixed data streams. Harry suddenly sat forward in his chair, staring at the holovision.

"You mean he can go into either VRE at will?" he asked, both shocked and excited by the prospect at the same time.

"It seems so. But there's more. In a way, it's the most exciting opportunity of all, and perhaps our biggest headache." Harry sat back, relaxing his whole body, letting his mind free up to cope with what he was learning. He had a fair idea what was coming next, and a small smile of anticipation started to form in spite of his efforts to hold it back. His friend, Freddie Fosdyke, had out smarted them all!

"In a nutshell, Fosdyke created a miniature portable generator, powered by a minute radiated crystal. He not only can go to any VRE at will, he can make and take his Virtual Reality Environment with him!" Captain Bellamy sat back, as if the effort of summarising the problem had drained all his strength. Harry nodded, finally understanding why his friend had been so hard to locate, and therefore so brutally destroyed.

"By "killing" him so publicly in Minendo, they reduced his hiding places by one, is that it?" he asked.

"Yes. What you don't know, is that Fosdyke managed to get himself into Duoendo as well."

"And they cut him down there too?"

"Violently. Even more dramatic than the first time. It seems that if you don't have a manbios to `lock' you into your VRE, you need some sort of electronic `key' to facilitate your existence, at least as seen and experienced by others. What they destroyed, along with Fosdyke's CGI, was this `key'. We've always know this, but it never seemed all that important before." Something at the back of Harry's agile mind started to tick, but he couldn't quite put his finger on it.

"Then that leaves him somewhere in the O/S?" Harry asked. And for the third time, the two Presidential Aides did their snake-eye trick in unison, and Harry's heart started to beat faster as the implications sunk in. He looked at Marion Harper, then at Captain Bellamy, and their air of expectation confirmed his hunch.

"So Freddie's loose somewhere in the O/S, but as a CGI, carrying his very own VRE around with him?" he asked softly, working through the possibilities of such a feat. If the CGI was good enough, Fosdyke was literally unstoppable, unless they fluked on his Corporeal form. And that could be living or stored anywhere on the remaining surface of the Earth. For that matter, there was no guarantee that there was only the one VR Freddie Fosdyke!

Incredible!

"Have you tried to find his Corporeal form?" he finally asked.

"Of course. But without opening every Cryogenic crib, digging up every grave, and physically body ID-ing every human left, there's no possible way of finding him." Harry seemed to withdraw into himself, his image partially thinning, as if had turned side-on to the four humans, or someone had reduced his available power.

"How does this portable VRE of his work?" he asked, filling out to full size again.

"It takes a "snap-shot" of the three-sixty degree horizon every five milliseconds, then creates a scaled reflection around the CGI of Fosdyke. Anyone looking at or interfacing with him sees what they expect to see - a human looking form interacting with the surrounding environment. Since the wavelength of our natural light has changed so much, the minute flicker you can sometimes see around a Computer Generated Image looks just like you'd expect around a normal Corporeal form. It's virtually undetectable." Marion Harper sat back in her chair, fascinated with the speed Harry was absorbing and analysing what he was hearing for the first time. A very unique mind, she thought to herself, momentarily sorry that their liaison three standard years before had only lasted such a short while.

Perhaps there would be possibilities in the future? She shuddered, inwardly frightened of what this thought really meant to her. Harry saw her reaction, but couldn't fathom its cause.

"But you can pick it if you know what to look for?" he asked her, smiling to ease her tension.

"Where to look, more than what to look for. The time-fold the VRE creates at the base of the CGI image leaves a tiny rippling effect, like a small wave hitting the edge of a pond. If you're not wearing Polaroid glasses, you can see it under his feet when he moves."

"Trouble is, what with the frequency change of our light, if you don't wear the Polaroids, you go blind," one of the Presidential Aides added. Harry adopted his thinking pose again, then his image turned towards Captain Bellamy.

"When did he visit you?" he asked, smiling at the thought. He could imagine that Fosdyke's presence would have sent the blood temperature of the two Presidential Aides sky-high. The crusty Captain had the good grace to laugh, knowing when he had been caught out in a deliberate omission.

"Yesterday. That's your this morning. Walked into headquarters as bold as brass, and asked for us to establish a link to you."

"Did you question him?"

"Tried to. He seemed very agitated, mumbled most of the time, said that he needed you to help calm us down, and communicate. That he had solved some problem or other he had been working on, and needed your help to make it work."

"What did you tell him?" Harry asked, curious as to why Fosdyke had sought him out specifically, after such a long absence.

"At first we thought he was in Corporeal form, and tried to restrain him. We threw a force-field cancellor at him, then tried physical restraint. You can guess the rest." Harry laughed, imagining the shock of the Police when they flew at Fosdyke, only to fall through his CGI straight into the hard concrete floor of Police Headquarters.

"What happened then?"

"Fosdyke took a second or two to realise what we had attempted. That confused us for a while, then we realised just how smart he was." Harry looked confused, trying to work this new wrinkle out. Then he got it.

"He used a time-shifted GCI on you?" he asked incredulously.

"Yes. Seems he was time-streaming in three locations at once, and was caught out when we did something unexpected. His attention was somewhere else." Harry suddenly had a flash of inspiration, and his image seemed to glow with renewed energy.

"You're running Duoendo at a different time-rate to Minendo," he stated, excited by the fantastic opportunities that such a development would open up. The two Presidential Aides lurched forward at the same time, then, again in unison, sat back in their chairs. They had been forewarned that Harry was the smartest Cop to ever migrate, but the speed with which he had guessed, or deduced, such accurate responses was phenomenal. Had they remembered that Harry's time-frame was running at half theirs, in effect, giving him just one relative second for every two of their standard ones, they would have been even more shocked.

"Yes. We've had a major breakthrough in that regard. Duoendo runs at one tenth normal time. You are experiencing half-rate, so you can imagine the enormity of this technical achievement." Harry was suddenly elated and shocked, both at the same time. Slowing the VRE's down to that level meant that he would still be functional in a hundred and fifty standard years, around about the time the Scientists estimated that the Earth would have cooled sufficiently for Corporeal life to resume on its surface. But if his Corporeal form had been disposed of, then he would have nothing to "go" back to.

Unless.......

And suddenly he understood the magnitude of Fosdyke's invention - and the reason why someone was so dedicated to taking it from him, at whatever cost. He decided to keep this revelation to himself for the time being, momentarily unsure of who to trust with it.

"Can you apply this new time-frame to Minendo?" he asked. Marion Harper shrugged, almost casually, as if the issue was of no real importance.

"Of course. Once you're stored as an electronic manbio, we can speed you up, slow you down, or even transfer you between VRE's if we have to."

"But it's the speed the Virtual Reality is running at that dictates the pace of the manbios, isn't it?" Marion Harper gave his image a shrewed look, pleased at his technical knowledge.

"Yes," she answered, "it is." Harry nodded. Another piece of the puzzle fell into place. If Fosdyke could control his time-stream, then he could jump from VRE to VRE no matter what speed they were running at, so long as his image and his "instant" surroundings were synchronised. The critical issue then, was how he had, or was going to, store his Corporeal form for the duration of the Earth's blow-up, for it was now quite obvious that this is what he intended.

"Tell me all about Kent and his two councillors," Harry asked, now more than satisfied with the progress of the case. With any luck, he would be out of this decidedly unfriendly standard time-stream and back into his own life-lengthening one before dinner time, and free of all the attendant drama.

Captain Bellamy snapped a holovision on, and the three dimensional shape of Ronald Kent warped into view. At the base of the image, the data Harry had already reviewed back in Minendo rippled by, until it reached a point in current standard time.

"You already know he migrated in 1999, month one. Before that he was Chief-of-Staff at the VRA where you did your orientation and conversion."

"Why was he instructed to migrate? By whom? And who allocated him to Commissioner status in Minendo?" Harry watched the two Presidential Aides carefully, waiting for them to give themselves away. He thought he had already guessed most of it, and was inwardly pleased when the good Captain confirmed it for him, the same split second their snake-eyed routine went into overtime.

"He had advanced radical cancer, the same type that is killing off most of the population. At the time he migrated, he had less than seven standard weeks to live. It was pretty close as it was." Harry nodded, only too well aware of the problems experienced with the electronic imprinting of a manbios from a Corporeal form that had degenerated beyond a certain point. "As for the who, it was his brother. Kent was appointed to the VRA by the President, then granted migration status. His job as Commissioner had been promised to him as part of his original deal."

"Once a power broker, always a power broker," mumbled Harry, starting to see the logic of the whole mess. He focussed on the Captain, forcing himself to appear calm. He didn't want the Aides to get wind of how much he had guessed. "Okay, one last little point. I take it that there is still only the one sure way of storing a healthy Corporeal form for the duration?" he asked. Marion Harper's eyelids fluttered quickly, then steadied down to her usual seductive glare. She glanced at the Captain as he answered, as if they shared a secret the Presidential Aides didn't.

"Yes. Cryogenic Cribs, either thrown into orbit, or stored in a heat-stable environment. But even then we believe that the radiation levels will eventually rise so high, that nothing will stop them. Why?"

"Just checking. I need to think this through, can you send me back?" he asked. The Captain looked at the Aides, then at Marion Harper. He finally shrugged his shoulders.

"Take as long as you need. And keep in touch." The Captain shimmered, disappeared, and suddenly Harry was back on his disc, shooting downwards at a blur. He evolved next to his desk, shook himself as if he were getting rid of errant raindrops, then sat down in his chair, carefully placing his long legs across the top of his untidy desk.

"Hi ya, boss!" Angie Valmorbida's face swam into view, and Harry turned to look at his monitor.

"Angie, what's up?"

"I gotta all thata info you wanted."

"Give it to me short."

" 'hokay. Fosdyke's movements for any month. Harry, they all the same. He's at the core for twelve days, then disappears for ten, back for twelve, then goes again."

"Where to?"

"No idea. Just disappears. No register of him at City Hall, no EMS monitors, nothing." Harry nodded slowly, starting to see a pattern in Fosdyke's movements.

"Who gives out the jobs in Minendo?" he asked.

"No-one. It'sa like you said. When you get here, you already know what you gonna do."

"Thanks, Angie, you can go home. Catch up on some sleep."

" 'hokay boss, see ya!" Angie's smiling face retracted into a pin-point of light, leaving Harry's screen strangely empty. He thought for a few more minutes, then pulled an ancient tattered notebook over, and drawing an even older old-fashioned fountain pen out of his jacket pocket, started to write copious notes, shedding all the data he had absorbed onto the lined yellow pages. For once, he was truly happy with the incredible detail the VRE of Minendo provided him with. It was almost like living back out in the O/S before his forced migration. He found himself smiling as he worked, pleased that he had a hard angle on the case, and even more pleased at the ramifications of the case itself.

Perhaps there could be worthwhile life after death, after all!

Captain Bellamy turned to Marion Harper, and handed her a strong Scotch on-the-rocks. "What do you think?"

She studied him for a full minute, her eyes noting the small, almost invisible brown blotches on his face that hinted at the rampant disease that was slowly consuming his intestines. "He'll work it out. Weather or not he comes up with something than can help us, I'm not sure. But he sure is fast." She tilted the cut crystal glass to her lips, allowing the mellow spirit to roll over her tongue, and slowly down her throat.

"We need to find Fosdyke. We need to hold off the President. And we need to be able to control a VRE from within, completely isolated and independent from any interference from outside." The Captain saw the sparkle of energy in Marion's eyes as she absorbed his summary, and not for the first time he thanked his lucky stars that God had given him such a beautiful and clever sister.

"Harry put his foot right on it when he asked me about the Cryogenic cribs. As soon as he works out that the only true alternative is an electronic Corporeal form, stored in the same VRE as the manbios, he'll be off and running."

The Captain sighed, his form suddenly seeming to deflate, and he slumped down into a leather chair, his body hugged by its rich tanned folds. "By God, I hope so. What he doesn't know is that we've only got about four months left before we all migrate or die, once and for all." She looked deep into her glass, as if seeking guidance in the swirls and sparkles the amber spirit made as it rippled over the odd-shaped ice cubes.

"If anyone can do it, Harry can. We'd better be ready for him," she said, turning to look fully at the Captain, her hazel eyes electric with contained energy. As one of the very few humans left that had not yet been struck by one of the new crop of virulent diseases, she radiated health and vitality, in direct contrast to those around her who were propped up by drugs and chemicals.

The Captain nodded, accepting her judgement. He reached for his miniature phone, and called the main Computer Laboratory. With any luck, the first prototype of what was to be known as a "Manbiot" should be ready soon for his inspection. Hopefully, before he either was forced to migrate to one of the VRE's, or he died.

He idly wondered if he would like living in it as much as Harry obviously enjoyed living in Minendo, and if the two of them would ever manage to share the same Environment again.

The little man's face swam into Harry's vision, finally settling into the regular frame of the monitor. Harry's feet, as usual, propped on the desk top, cut off a small corner of the screen, so he shifted them to one side and leaned slightly forward in his chair. The little man smiled, outwardly quite relaxed, but the small lines that flowed from the corner of his twinkling eyes twitched nervously, giving away his inner turmoil.

He knew Harry had something on him, but he didn't know what.

"Can I help you?" he asked, just the faintest flutter in his voice. Harry stared straight back at the image, letting the tension build. He had decided on his strategy over breakfast, and without hesitation, let the little man know just how much trouble he was in.

"I'll make it quick. I'm not interested in your illegal use of the ROMBIOS. Or your scam with the O/S. But if you don't immediately help me, I'll have your manbios pulled, and cancelled without notice." Harry let the threat sink in, then pushed his obvious advantage. "I want immediate contact with Freddie, on his own, as a singleton, in any form or VRE he chooses. Private and confidential, just between him and me. Can you do it?"

"Erh, yes. At least, I can contact him. But I can't guarantee that he will do what you ask." Naked fear rippled across the little man's eyes, as the finality of Harry's threat reached deep down into his memory core. With his Corporeal form disposed of five standard years ago, without his manbios, his electronic "personality", he would cease to exist in any plane, forever, irretrievably. Something that didn't bear thinking about.

"Then you had better do your best." Harry snapped the monitor off, and sat back, stretching to place his linked hands behind his head. He expected action, and got it.

The stars of the Southern Milky Way swam into view, as the spaceship gradually rolled around its spine, keeping each face of its huge surface continually moving in and out of the deadly carcinogenic rays being emitted by the blue-white dwarf Star that now almost totally blocked the Sun. Known simply as "Alpeaso-113", after the Spanish Astronomer who had first sighted, and claimed due credit, for the greatest and possibly final discovery of the twentieth and twenty-first centuries, the Star loomed large in everyone's mind. Where it had come from, deep beyond the edges of the viewable universe, no-one knew. It had just appeared from behind a massive undiscovered black hole one day, on a two hundred year orbit of destruction.

Funny thing was, it was smaller in mass than the Earth's Moon, but threatened the Earth in a way that had previously been thought impossible. Like a flaming out of control comet, Alpeaso-113 moved inexorably closer every minute, sucking the very life out of humanity with its sheer atomic brilliance.

"I thought you'd like to see this," Freddie said, handing Harry a weightless sucking-straw attached to a drink bladder. Harry sucked some of the pale pink fluid, noticing the faint smell of almonds. If this was an artificially generated virtual reality environment, it was a very good one.

"Thanks. But how in hell are you doing this? Captain Bellamy said that the only other VRE that has been successfully built, was a similar Environment to Minendo." Harry looked at his friend, lying back in a mild-gravity hammock, seemingly absorbed with the outside view of deep space. Suddenly Freddie smiled, as if remembering an enormous joke.

"You always were a super-straight!" he laughed, and with no discernible effort warped them both into another VRE, this time a sparsely fitted-out Winnebago, parked high on a cliff overlooking the ocean. From the position of the sun, with its ever present, ever growing black spot, Harry guessed that they were somewhere on the edge of the Pacific ocean, and that meant that they were probably somewhere on the Southern coast of California. Harry went to suck on his drink, only to find that he now held a Tom-Collins in a crystal goblet, with green mint and a small umbrella hanging over one side. He hid his surprise, and sipped slowly, watching his former friend from over the rim of the weighty glass.

As a cop, and a good one, he had learned the value of patience, and how to control his emotions. It had stood him in good stead during his long career.

"Harry, compared to what I can do, Minendo is like a bitter-sweet piece of ancient history." He stood up, and walked in a slight crouch to a well fitted video entertainment system, and reached for a small black infra-red controller.

"You're real!" Harry shouted, so startled he dropped his drink, which promptly spilt all over his lap, spreading a mottled stain over his otherwise grubby coat. Fredrick Fosdyke smiled, nodding slowly, waiting for his friend to catch his metaphorical breath.

"Yes, I am. And that should tell you something about the power of my invention." Harry stopped his mopping up, eyebrows furrowed in concentration.

"This is not a VRE. It's real, too," he said in a hushed voice, hardly believing his own eyes.

"Right again. But you needn't worry, I've got you wrapped securely in a three-sixty VRE that exactly matches this reality, so you shouldn't feel too out of place." Harry sat back into his seat, the implications of his experience temporarily overwhelming him. It was one thing to live in a VRE, permanently, but quite another to suddenly find yourself back on the O/S, as nothing more substantial than a holographically projected computer generated image.

"But how do you do it? And why aren't you .........." his voice trailed off as his capricious mind finally caught up with the situation. He smiled, radiating sudden warmth and confidence, proud of his friend and his mighty achievement, yet scared to the very synthetic marrow of his bones by its implications. "I get it now, you bastard, I get it now. And now I know why everyone wants your body!" His forehead suddenly creased in concentration as a stray thought crossed his mind.

As if reading Harry's very thoughts, Freddie shook his head. "No, they can't tap into your manbios and read this, or track us, for that matter, I've locked them out. That's a by-product of the process." Harry stared at his friend, open-mouthed, the opportunities mind-boggling, even for him.

"Well I guess I'll have to take you in then," he said, grinning from ear to ear, seeing the funny side of a CGI who only now existed as a computer code in a VRE, trying to apprehend a real live human being!

"I think we need to talk first, then you should go off on your own. I'll join you when they get a little more used to the idea." Harry thought about it for a standard second or two, realised that he had little ability to actually influence Freddie, or do anything but look and learn, and decided to go on his hunch. Freddie had always felt "right" to him, one reason why they had struck up such a firm friendship in the O/S prior to their VRA experience.

"Okay, play it your way. Just don't disappear on me," he said, forcing a stern look to underline his seriousness.

"Don't worry, Harry, I won't let you down. If it hadn't been for you, I wouldn't have fluked onto this process in the first place." Freddie turned up the volume on an old Western Song called "Mississippi Blue Grass", and the two men hunkered down, one to discover the future form of the human race, the other to try and bargain for the rest of his very life, both real and generated.

"It's all about power and control," Harry flatly stated, refusing to grace any of the twenty or so self-confessed Very Important People in the room with a direct look. He was counting on keeping them edgy, a little off-balance, because he had precious little to go on, in real terms, just the observations of an out-of-control genius, and the experience of a computer generated Cop, living out his days in an artificially created Reality. Not an awe-inspiring combination, he thought to himself with a rueful smile, but it was all he had, so he gave it his best shot. Angie Valmorbida fidgeted nervously next to him, and the Captain and Marion Harper sat mute just off to one side, happy to watch what eventuated.

The VRE that had been specially created for the occasion, in keeping with the original Third Law of Virtual Reality, "Any Interface between a manbios and a Corporeal Being must take place in a Virtual Reality Environment", was an old fashioned Court Room, set up as it was in the days of Congressional Investigations. Someone had a warped sense of humour. The President, his wife, several Aides, the Chief-of-Staff, the Joint

Chiefs' Representative, and the heads of Army, Navy, Airforce, Marines and Special Services were there, along with a private recording Engineer and thirty odd Scientists from the two VRA projects - Minendo, and Duoendo. Now that the Earth was literally fighting for its life, squabbles between different Countries and Political Factions was almost nonexistent, but old habits died hard, and the Military still tried to stick their bib into anything that looked interesting, just in case an opportunity came up where they could score valuable points in the who-would-live and who-would-die game now being played out.

"As you all appreciate, even now, none of you are really comfortable talking to a computer created image. I know, I felt the same way before I went through the VRA." Harry let the rumble of disagreement die down, as the Military Men tried to outdo the Government Civil Servants in forced bravado. Fact was, even with the superb conditioning of the Virtual Reality Academy, and after nearly six standard years of actually "living" in a VRE, somewhere not too far from the centre of his being, a dark, nasty, uncomfortable thought still lurked in the hidden recesses of Harry's brain. The kind of thought that screaming, kicking, sweating sanity killing nightmares are made of.

"Now, as we all know, the issue that is forcing us all to accept the limitations of migration to VRE's for survival is the inability of the human body to withstand the incredibly virulent cancers and mutated diseases that have been produced by the radiation of Alpeaso-113, the white dwarf Star that suddenly popped up out of nowhere, and now looks like being around for about two hundred standard years or so." Several heads nodded in agreement, happy that Harry was as last talking facts, not feelings. "According to Marion Harper, as of 0300 hours standard time today, there are less than five million corporeal beings on the Earth that are not yet affected by mutated radiation-induced diseases. However, this figure is degrading by 8% daily, as I understand it, giving you just four to five months before there will be literally no human body alive that is unaffected, not carrying some malignancy to some degree or other."

The silence in the room was deafening, and given that the human beings were constrained in a comfort couch, with a weighty helmet strapped to their heads, in order to be able to participate in the created Virtual Reality, this was no small achievement! Harry continued, watching closely to see who would give themselves away first. "However, we all know that for a corporeal being to be successfully migrated to a VRE, the disease-state cannot be too far advanced, or the neural-synapses are so screwed up that a "healthy" personality cannot be imprinted on a manbios - the computer chip that makes all this possible in the first place." Again, several heads nodded in agreement. "And we all know what that means."

"Physical death," muttered one of the Military men, as if he were speaking a dreaded curse against his will.

"Yes, total cessation of the physical, mental, and spiritual being, at least as you know it on the O/S."

"What's this got to do with someone killing off manbios in Minendo?" snapped the President, finally unable to hold onto his temper. As Harry had since worked out for himself, the President was dying, and apparently quite quickly, making his migration to a VRE or some other substitute existence all that more urgent.

"Quite a lot, Mister President, quite a lot. If you will just give me a little time to set this all up for you, I'm sure you'll agree that it was worth the wait." Harry stared directly at the President, whose eyes glowed with suppressed fury. As the elected President of the United States just four years in office, he was having great difficulty in balancing the enormous power he could wield over affairs-of-State, with the almost total lack of control he had over the rapid degeneration of his body, and the inevitable crumbling of the civilisation he had held so dear to his heart for all of his adult life. He nodded curtly, motioning for Harry to continue with a withering hand.

"As we interface right now, at this moment, you are all constrained on a comfort couch, with a computer-linked biosynaptic brain helmet surrounding your head. Correct?" All the heads in the room nodded, some with a smile, others with a grimace.

The helmet weighed nearly one hundred pounds, more than a human could easily support unless lying down, and even then, it was by no means a comfortable experience. "The problem with VRE's has always been that once you are imprinted onto a manbios, there's no way back into corporeal form." Again all heads nodded in agreement, as this was the major issue that had perplexed a dying world, from President to Pope to ordinary man in the street. On the one hand, you could "live" out a useful life inside a computer, hidden deep in the bowels of the earth somewhere, while on the other your flesh and bones were disposed of like so much garbage, never to be revisited again.

"Now, because of the fact that the Earth's surface will soon become, literally, an uninhabitable boiling cauldron for around one hundred and fifty years, it's been agreed by International Convention to dispose of the corporeal form of any personality who is successfully imprinted onto a manbios." Silence again, followed by a scratching noise as someone shifted their position, the bionic helmet amplifying their uncomfortable thoughts for all to share. On cue, Angie leaned slowly forward, resting his projected arms on the top of the decorative Attorney's bench.

"Nowa, Mister President, howa would you like ita if you could live down here with us, but still keepa your corporeal form in the O/S?" he asked, allowing Harry to scrutinise all the eyes in the room for the slightest give-away twitch of fore-knowledge.

"But that's impossible," exploded the President, starting to stand, then, remembering who he was and where he was, folded back down into his seat. "Firstly, no-one can protect themselves from the mutated cancers, and secondly, nothing that we've made or constructed can withstand the super heating of the Earth's surface." The angry faces of the Military men lent support, and for a fleeting moment Harry hoped he had got it right. Marion Harper came to his immediate rescue, and with an edge to her voice that belayed any protest.

"Absolutely correct, Mister President. But just suppose for a moment that a healthy person could be protected from the radiation diseases. What then?" Every head in the room turned to look at the President, as if he had the answer to the most important question on Earth, which, in a sense, he did.

"Then," he drawled, scratching his chin, his hands trembling with the thought, "the Space Habitats would come into their own. We could populate the Stars, and, hopefully, repopulate the Earth in centuries to come."

"Exactly." Harry looked at the faces of the most powerful men still alive on the O/S, knowing now that his instincts, and his gut-driven deductions were spot on. "Space has always been the attractive solution, but the radiation from the white dwarf is too intense, and defies any form of shielding we have come up with."

"Cryogenic storage is only as good as the possibility of someone existing in two hundred years to reverse the process," offered Angie, feeling the first sparks of energy flow through the room as Harry zeroed in on his target. "Not to mention the risk of either radiation or heat contamination during the two hundred years they are stored."

"And an existence within a VRE is all one way," finished Marion Harper, "once you're imprinted on a manbios, that's it as far as a corporeal existence is concerned."

"What about your experiments with robots and the like?" fired back the President.

"Still limited, and will eventually be only as good as we can make them now, because there'll be no-one alive in two hundred years to make them better."

"I see." The President scratched his chin again, then turned the full force of his azure blue eyes on the image of Harry. "Your partner asked me a question. Does that presuppose that you have the answer?" he asked.

"Yes. But to convince you, I need your indulgence."

"What for?" asked one of the Presidential Aides who had been present in the Captain's office. The President waved him down, gesturing to Harry.

"You have it. But it had better be good." Harry smiled, knowing that he had his fish on the hook, and now all he had to do was reel him in gently.

"Thank you, Sir. Angie, when you're ready." Angie nodded, and switched on a holograph, throwing a massive multidimensional image into the centre of the court room, out of which the body and smiling face of Fredrick Fosdyke emerged. He bowed towards the President, bobbing his head.

"Mister President, Ladies and Gentlemen, thank you for your time." Three of the Military men and both Presidential Aides leapt to their feet, then hastily sat down again when they realised that all they were seeing was a projected image, within a Virtual Reality!

"The mysterious Fredrick Fosdyke," the President said, looking towards Harry. "Well done, Mister Roberts, well done!" Harry ignored the compliment, gesturing for Freddie to sit down, which he did, with rare elegance and style.

"Mister President, I said earlier that this case is all about power and control. I meant just that." Harry stood, and walked slowly towards the holograph of Freddie, sitting relaxed in what would have been the witness chair in days of old. "You see, my friend here, way back in 1994, discovered a better way to make and project VRE's. But no one would take any notice."

"Back in 1994 the World was panicking after the discovery of the white dwarf," the President interjected.

"Exactly. VRE's were the domain of the Japanese and parlour games. Then Japan suddenly disappeared in a volcanic upheaval, and it was left to Silicon Valley to perfect the techniques."

"Which they did."

"Which they most assuredly did. What, with billions of dollars of Government money, the whole might of the Military-Industrial Complex behind them, they did twenty years work in two, resulting in the successful migration of fifty thousand manbios to Minendo."

"And the development of Duoendo," added the President. Harry nodded, pleased with his progress so far.

"Yes. And the covert development of at least six more VRE's that you don't know about." The room suddenly erupted, people standing then sitting, standing then, in frustration with the severe limits of their participation in the Virtual Reality Environment of the old Court House, sitting again. Harry waited until the hubbub died down, then motioned to Angie.

"There are sixa VRE's, running ona different time frames, orbiting the Earth righta now in Military Satellites," Angie stated, enjoying immensely the shock reflected on the faces of all the so-called Very Important People in the room. "Eacha one has a booster attached, and is easily capable of getting up into a geo-stationary orbit ata some time ina the future." Harry waited for Angie's news to sink in, then delivered what he hoped would be a telling blow to the conspirators, for that is what he had come to see them as.

"And in loose synchronous orbit with those satellites are six habitats large enough to hold about one thousand corporeal forms in permanent cyrongenic storage," he added, watching the Military men get even more and more uncomfortable.

"The radiation will kill them, destroy them, before they can be regenerated." The sad way the President said it left Harry in no doubt that he already knew about the satellites. And the lack of response by the Presidential Aides this time made it obvious that what they had planned was one type of VRE for the VIP's, and the other type for the rest. He sighed, suddenly depressed with the thought that even in Man's greatest time of need, there was going to be a false discrimination in the way the survivors would try to live through the disaster. He shrugged his shoulders, there was nothing he could do about it, indeed, it was still up to those on the O/S to maintain and guarantee the survival of the existing VRE's as it was.

An uncomfortable thought at the best of times, which this wasn't. Time to move on.

"What if you could protect the stored bodies from the radiation?" He asked.

"Impossible! That has been researched over and over since day one. No-one's even come close."

"I have."

Every head in the room snapped towards Fredrick Fosdyke, the almost forgotten man in the tense discussion between the two Cops and the President.

"You have what?" demanded the President.

"I have found a way to protect a human being from the radiation." Stunned silence flooded the room, and for a brief second not even the normal background static of the electronic imagers could be heard. Freddie got up from his seat, and walked slowly towards the table that Harry and Angie were seated at. At almost the same time, another image of Freddie formed behind the President, and started to walk down the isle between the Presidential party and the Military men.

"You see, Mister President, not everything in life comes to those with the biggest cheque books. Freddie has the ability to exist in any VRE, and remain in corporeal form, all at the same time. Further more, and I've seen this with my own eyes, Freddie's corporeal form can survive in cryogenic storage for the duration, without him having to be imprinted on a manbios!" A cascade of shouts and comments broiled around the room, finally settling down into a dull roar of protest. Here was the Holy Grail, the harbinger of Life, and some crazy nobody had control of it! Incredible, unbelievable, and totally unsustainable. One by one the Military men snapped out of the VRE, no doubt to immediately trace Freddie's electronic footprint. Harry smiled to himself. Let them try.

"Originally, Mister President, we believed that once a manbios was imprinted, and the personality successfully migrated to a VRE, the corporeal form had to be disposed of because there was no known way of maintaining it free from radiation poisoning." Marion Harper paused to catch her breath, amused as the Military men snapped back into the VRE, obviously furious that they had found no way to exercise control over the precedings, or the two Cops and Freddie Fosdyke. The good Captain had seen to that by isolating their power supply, and hiding their manbios in his portable computer, which was safely tucked away under his inert form in the comfort couch.

"But if you can protect the cryogenic cribs, then we can hope for a rebirth!" The President was agitated, he kept thinking that he had other things to do, even though none were as important as the implications of this meeting.

"Yes Sir, but only if we devise a way to re-enter the corporeal form." The two images of Freddie Fosdyke now stood side by side next to Harry, facing the President. One stood perfectly still, while the other became quite animated.

"And I can do that, Mister President, if only you and your goons would stop hunting me down and wasting my time!" he shouted, pointing at the President. "Three times I tried to give you, and the people, the results of my research, and three times you threw it back in my face. Well, now it's too late." His voice thundered around the court room just as his image snapped out of the VRE, leaving just the ghost of a memory behind. Harry stood up, leaning forward on his knuckles.

"Mister President, I'll leave it for you to establish which of your Aides, and which of your Military men have betrayed you. Your brother and his two henchmen have already paid the ultimate price for their duplicity, how, I won't go into at this time. Although, God knows, you have betrayed us all equally as much. But understand this," he said, as Angie stood up beside him, "before we entered the VRA we were guaranteed certain things. Rules were formed, and agreed to, to protect our existence. In return, we were to provide a fast-track learning experience for those of you who followed. By attempting to create your own Environments, at the expense of the people, you have ultimately betrayed our trust. What ever happens to you now, you deserve!" And they both snapped out of the VRE together, leaving the second image of a laughing Freddie standing in isolation next to the empty desk.

"Harry, I've got a call for you," the pretty operator said, breaking into his thoughts. It was forty relative days since he had confronted the President and his men, and he had heard nothing of the consequences of the meeting. He used his wrist controller to light up his monitor, swinging around on his chair to look into its dull surface.

"Hello Harry."

"Captain." Neither man smiled, obviously submerged in their own thoughts.

"You've got a new migrant intake, and I want you to go meet them."

"Why? There's a procedure for that."

"Just do it!" The look on Captain Bellamy's face left Harry in no doubt about the outcome of the argument, so he shrugged his shoulders, snapping the controller off. He walked disconsolately out to his floater, dialled in the necessary map reference, and settled back to let the little car do its job. Nothing felt the same, now that he had discovered that the O/S was running their own agenda. He had lost confidence in his future, in the future for any of the manbios in Minendo or any other VRE, for that matter. If they were to be manipulated by the O/S, there was little they could do to stop it. The whole game depended on trust and belief, and since the Court House meeting, Harry had precious little of that left.

Even in the most technically brilliant time of mankind, the simplest human traits of honesty, trust, and mutual dependency dominated the mind of man.

He stepped out of the floater, looked up at the imposing facade of City Hall, and slowly walked up the fifty one steps, one for each of the States he and the other manbios had left behind in the O/S.

"Mister Roberts!" called a tall, lanky man, hidden in the shadows of the reception area.

"Mister President!" Harry replied, genuinely surprised as the lanky man came into the light. Harry reluctantly accepted the outstretched hand, unsure of his feelings.

"Let's go for a walk," the President said, capping Harry on his shoulder, and steering him back outside. The two men negotiated the stairs, the paused, while the President made a show of sniffing the air, searching the bright blue sky for familiar contrails from high-flying jets. "Ahh, it's just as the book says. You truly are reborn!" He started off down the street, Harry slow to catch up. The President paused again at a rocky mound, on which had been placed an old wrought-iron lattice bench. He indicated with one hand, and seeing a flicker of interest in Harry's eyes, sat down. Harry joined him, although at a slight distance.

"I must say, Mister President, you're looking a lot better than the last time we met." The President gave him a searching look, then smiled.

"Yes, I am, aren't I?". He seemed to be considering his next words, his hands suddenly fidgeting. "Harry, Marion Harper explained to me what you - that is, I am one now, too - but, erh, well, she explained how you all must feel in here with people on the O/S able to manipulate you at will." He stared into Harry's soul, holding his eyes with the sheer force of his sincerity.

"It doesn't feel good, if that's what you mean." The President nodded.

"Harry, I'm sorry. You can't imagine the pressures that are on the Office of the President. You have no idea just how twisted everything can get with all those well-meaning people yapping at you. Your priorities seem to change by the minute!"

"And now?" Harry asked, thawing slightly, his gut still in a turmoil from the constant stress of worrying for the past five relative weeks about his future.

"And now, I've joined you down here in Minendo. I didn't have a choice, of course, at least, not as to when I migrated. But I could have chosen any of the VRE's available, including the ones in space." Harry leaned back on the cool metal bench, enjoying the psudo-physicalness of it sticking into his back and shoulders.

"Why Minendo? We go the fastest, we're the oldest, and from what I understand from Freddie, the hardest to change." The President nodded, a small smile spreading across his tanned face.

"All true, all true. But with me here, I think some priorities might be shifted, don't you?" he asked. Harry turned to look directly at the President, in his new form, at least twenty years younger looking than he had been in the Court House.

"But you have no more control in the O/S than any of us do," he said quietly, crossing his legs.

"Ahh, but I do. And it's all to do with your friend Freddie!" The President laughed, slapped Harry on the back, and stood up, forcing Harry to join him. "Harry, with your talent as a Cop, your friend Fredrick's genius, and with my political clout, we can go to the Stars. Do you want to know how?" Harry looked puzzled, then suddenly relaxed. It was a beautiful day, and his Cop's gut told him that this tall, rangy new migrant standing opposite him was clean, probably even telling the truth. Or at the very worst, what he believed to be the truth. Harry shrugged his shoulders, thrusting his hands deep down into his pockets.

"Why not?" he said, setting off down the street. One hundred yards behind, like a good electrodog, his floater silently rose up off the footpath, and discretely followed.

Harry looked over his shoulder and smiled, as a fleeting thought flashed through his brain. Some things never change!

The moral of this story is simple -
no matter how great the challenge,
no matter how great the perceived barriers,
and no matter how seemingly
impossible the task,
it will always come down
to one person saying -
"I will, I do, I did,
and I am accountable!"

But then, would you have it any other way?

# THE END AND THE BEGINNING

All good things
must come to an end,
even a book like this.
But take heart,
there's more to be had,
and it's yours for the taking!

As the Chairman of the largest population on Earth once said, "A journey of a thousand miles starts with a single step", so too does your journey start.

Where it will end, only you can determine. How powerful you will become, only you and your intellect can decide.

And what you do with your personal power once developed, will ultimately determine your destiny.

In times to come, when things do not look as they really are, remember the creed of the simple Man who is to be counted.

"I will, I do, I did,
and I am Accountable!

If you are, and if you do, and then if you did, and you are accountable, then you can never fail in anything you ever strive for, and your achievements will truly be great!

I know you will not fail, and wish you every success on the path to personal power.